The English Advantage

STUDENT BOOK
LEVEL TWO

Jacqueline Flamm

W. Leland Northam

Richard C. Yorkey

NewburyHouse
A Division of HarperCollins*Publishers*

For Alice and Doyle Lawrence, my parents, and all my students and colleagues over the years.
WLN

Director: Laurie E. Likoff
Development Editor: Patricia Nardiello
Full-Service Manager: Michael Weinstein
Production Coordinator: Cynthia Funkhouser
Text Design: Mary McDonnell/A Good Thing, Inc.
Cover Design: Mary McDonnell/A Good Thing, Inc.
Cover Illustration: Mary McDonnell/A Good Thing, Inc.
Photo Research: Julie Tesser
Production: Jeffrey Taub
Printer and Binder: Arcata/Kingsport

NEWBURY HOUSE
A division of HarperCollins Publishers

Language Science
Language Teaching
Language Learning

The English Advantage, Student Book, Silver

Library of Congress Cataloging-in-Publication Data

Flamm, Jacqueline, 1940–
The English advantage : student book, level two / Jacqueline Flamm, W. Leland Northam, Richard C. Yorkey.
p. cm.
Includes index.
ISBN 0-06-632625-7
1. English language—Textbooks for foreign speakers. I. Northam, W. Leland. II. Yorkey, Richard. III. Title.
PE1128.F5265 1991
428.2'4—dc20 90-13525
CIP

91 92 93 94 9 8 7 6 5 4 3 2

ACKNOWLEDGMENTS
The authors would like to thank the following people for their contributions: Laurie E. Likoff, Director of Newbury House Publishers; Patricia Nardiello, Development Editor; Joana Jebsen, Marketing Manager; Cynthia Funkhouser, Production Coordinator; Alida Greydanus, Editorial Coordinator; Jacqueline Rebisz, Editor; Paul Kirouac, Mary McDonnell, and Dianne Stetch, Designers, A Good Thing, Inc.; Louis Carrillo, Contributor; and the following professors, language specialists, and program directors who provided insightful comments through reviews, field-testing, and piloting of sample materials that immeasurably improved the final manuscript and contributed to its international perspective.

Professor Paul F. Abraham
English Language Institute
Bradford College
Bradford, MA

Dr. Marta M. Moreno
Department of English
University of Puerto Rico
Mayaguez, PR

Mrs. Celia Z. Rocha
Academic Coordinator
Instituto Brasil-Estados Unidos
Rio de Janeiro, Brazil

Professor Janis S. Perez
International Students' Program
Miami Dade Community College-South
Miami, FL

Ms. Ioko Fujiwara
Japan College of Foreign Languages
Tokyo, Japan

Mr. Hiroki Sato
Kyoto English Center
Kyoto, Japan

Catherine Cox
Academic Coordinator
Casa Thomas Jefferson
Brasilia, Brazil

Donald Occhiuzzo
Academic Director
Kathleen Harrington
General Coordinator
Department of English
ALUMNI
São Paulo, Brazil

Blanca Arazi
Director
Patricia Veciño
Academic Coordinator
Instituto Cultural Argentino Norteamericano
Buenos Aires, Argentina

Mary Oliveira
Academic Supervisor
Daniela Meyer
Academic Supervisor
IBEU
Rio de Janeiro, Brazil

Mr. Charles Sandy
Supervisor
Kanda Institute of Foreign Languages
Tokyo, Japan

Ms. Liliana Baltra
Instituto Chileno Norteamericano
Santiago, Chile

Ms. Maria de la Paz Pena
Department of Courses
Centro Cultural Paraguayo Americano
Asuncion, Paraguay

Prof. Martine Aceves-Foster
Kapiolani Community College
Honolulu, HI

Prof. Suma Kurien
English Language Center
LaGuardia Community College
Long Island City, NY

CONTENTS

INTRODUCTION

Richard: HELLO, EVERYONE. DO YOU REMEMBER US? WE'RE THE AUTHORS OF *THE ENGLISH ADVANTAGE*. WE'D LIKE TO WELCOME YOU TO THE SECOND BOOK, THE SILVER LEVEL

Jacqueline: WE HOPE YOU ENJOYED THE BRONZE LEVEL, AND...

Leland: WAIT A MINUTE. YOU CAN'T ASSUME THAT EVERYONE HAS READ THE FIRST BOOK, CAN YOU?

Jacqueline: WHAT DO YOU MEAN?

Leland: WELL, YOU CAN BEGIN *THE ENGLISH ADVANTAGE* WITH THIS LEVEL, CAN'T YOU?

Jacqueline: SURE, YOU CAN.

Richard: RIGHT. YOU DON'T HAVE TO START WITH THE FIRST LEVEL. THAT'S WHAT YOU MEAN, ISN'T IT?

Leland: YES, IT IS. SOME STUDENTS CAN BEGIN WITH THIS BOOK BECAUSE THEY ALREADY KNOW SOME ENGLISH.

Jacqueline: THAT'S TRUE. WELL, WE HAVE TO INTRODUCE OURSELVES AGAIN FOR THE PEOPLE WHO DIDN'T MEET US IN THE FIRST BOOK.

RY: Well, OK, I'll introduce myself first. I'm Richard Yorkey. I taught English for many years—in the Middle East, in Canada, and in the United States. Now I'm living in Vermont and writing textbooks. I'd like you to meet Leland Northam. He's from Alabama, but he lived in New York for a long time—about ten years, I think.

LN: Then I moved to Colombia a few years ago. I'm an English teacher with many years of experience. Now I'm a language consultant, and I write English language textbooks. Let me introduce you to Jacqueline Flamm. I met her when I was living in New York. That was a long time ago, wasn't it?

JF: Yes, it was—almost twenty years ago. But, I don't live in New York now. My husband and I are currently living in New Jersey—near Princeton. I began to teach English more than twenty-five years ago—in Washington, D.C. Then I went to Italy and I taught English as a Foreign Language there. I've known Dr. Yorkey and Mr. Northam for a long time. The three of us work very well together—long distance, of course!

LN: Patricia Nardiello, our editor, is over there. And this is Laurie Likoff, the director of Newbury House publishers.

LL: We think you'll find that this book is more interesting than the first one.

RY: That's because you know more English now.

JF: And the activities are more interesting.

LN: And the lessons are longer and more exciting.

LL: Remember to write to the authors. Tell them how you are enjoying the lessons. You can write to them even if you don't like the lessons. Your feedback can really help all of us! Our address is:

Newbury House, a division of HarperCollins Publishers Inc.
10 E. 53rd Street
New York, NY 10022

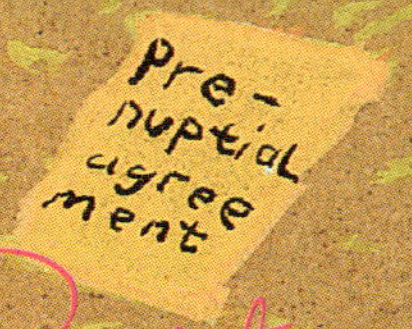

Lesson 41: The Engagement Party

Andy and Nancy . . .

Andy Jones is getting married. His friends are happy for him. But they are very surprised. Why? Because Andy has always said, "I'm not the marrying kind. I'm a free spirit." But then he met Nancy Ward. Now he's looking forward to his marriage. "Nancy is the perfect woman for me," he says.

Nancy lives in New York and works for a very large publishing company. She's an editor. She travels to Washington, D.C., about once a month. Andy is British, but he lives and works in Washington, D.C. He's a computer programmer and a teacher at a computer school. One weekend Nancy took a course in computer literacy and Andy was her teacher.

Andy is moving to New York soon. He's starting a new business to develop computer software. It's all very exciting—a new business, a new city, and a new life!

At the party . . .
JOE: Hi. My name is Joe Colombo. And you are . . .?
SUE: Hello, Joe. I'm Sue Parks. Uh, how do you know Andy and Nancy?
JOE: Well, I don't know Andy at all. I'm meeting him for the first time. I know Nancy from work. I'm an editor. How about you?
SUE: I know Andy from home. We're old friends.
JOE: Home? Where's home?
SUE: England. We're both originally from Cornwall.
JOE: And what are you doing in New York?
SUE: I'm on holiday for a fortnight. With my husband.
JOE: A two-week vacation! It's nice that you're here for the party.
SUE: Yes, it's a lucky coincidence, isn't it?
JOE: Yes, it is. Are you going to the wedding?
SUE: I'm not sure. Is there a wedding date?
JOE: They're thinking about December.
SUE: That's almost a year away!
JOE: They believe in long engagements.

THE INVITATION

Dr. and Mrs. Joseph Ward
request the honour[1] of your presence
at the marriage of their daughter
Nancy Lee
to
Mr. Andrew Nigel Jones
on
Saturday, the first of December
Nineteen hundred and ninety-one
at
eleven o'clock in the morning
The Northshore Country Club
Main Avenue
Northshore, Long Island, New York

THE GUEST

LOVE USA 25

Mr. Joseph Colombo
166 E. 34th Street
New York, New York 10016

THE RETURN ENVELOPE

LOVE USA 25

Dr. & Mrs. Joseph Ward
1415 Shore Drive
Northshore, NY 11733

TWO R.S.V.P.[2] CARDS

Please respond on or before
November 15, 1991
M r. Joseph Colombo
will ________ attend
with great pleasure

Please respond on or before
November 15, 1991
M r + Mrs Roger Parks
will not attend
Sorry! We'll be in England!

THE DIRECTIONS

Directions to the Northshore Country Club
From New York: Take the Long Island Expressway to Exit 41. Go north on Seaside Highway to Exit 4. Go east on Central Avenue to the second traffic light and turn right on Northshore Road. The Northshore Country Club is ½ mile on the right.

[1]American English equivalent: honor

[2]R.S.V.P. is an abbreviation for the French *répondez s'il vous plaît*. It is commonly used on invitations and means "please reply."

LESSON 42 Driving to Florida

Roger  and **Sue**  **Parks** are visiting the United States with their son and daughter, **Terry**  and **Amanda.** 

They have a two-week vacation. They're renting a car in New York and driving to Florida. They're staying with Sue's sister, Heather, who lives in Orlando with her husband and two children. Amanda and Terry Parks are going to Disney World with their cousins. This is their first trip to the United States. It's Sue's third trip. It's Roger's fifth or sixth trip. He doesn't remember exactly.

Friday the 31st: Arrive at J.F.K.[1]

Saturday the 1st: Go to the theatre[2] in the afternoon. Attend Andy's engagement party at the Plaza Hotel in the evening.

Sunday the 2nd: Spend the day in New York. Visit the Metropolitan Museum of Art, the Guggenheim Museum and the World Trade Center. If time permits, go to Chinatown and Little Italy.

Monday the 3rd: Rent a car. Drive to Philadelphia.[3] Visit Independence National Historical Park. Stay at the Hershey Hotel.

Tuesday the 4th: Drive to Washington D.C. Visit Mount Vernon,[4] the Washington Monument, the Lincoln Memorial, and the Jefferson Memorial. Stay at the Mayflower Hotel on Connecticut Avenue.

Wednesday the 5th: Visit the Air and Space Museum, the National Gallery of Art, the Smithsonian Institution.

Thursday the 6th: Drive to Williamsburg.[5]

Friday the 7th: Travel to Raleigh, North Carolina.

Saturday the 8th: Go to Charleston, South Carolina.

Sunday the 9th: Drive to Savannah, Georgia. Have lunch. Drive to Jacksonville, Florida.

Monday the 10th: Arrive in Orlando.

Tuesday the 11th: Rest, Relax, sleep.

Wednesday the 12th: Visit Disney World.

Thursday the 13th: Tour MGM's theme park.

Friday the 14th: Visit Epcot Center.

Saturday the 15th: Fly to Miami. Take British Airways to London.

[1]John Fitzgerald Kennedy International Airport-one of the three main airports in the New York City area.

[2]The American spelling is *theater*.

[3]The first capital of the United States and the birthplace of the U.S. Constitution.

[4]The home of George Washington, the first U.S. President.

[5]The restored colonial capital of Virginia (until 1780).

Terry and Amanda are writing a lot of postcards to their friends in England. Here are two:

Saturday
Dear Nick,
I'm having a super vacation (that's American for "holiday"). We saw The Phantom of the Opera[1] in New York. Tomorrow we're driving to Florida. We're stopping in Philadelphia, Washington, and some other places. It's very different here. They drive on the wrong side of the road! And they talk funny! (That's American for "peculiar.") Hope you're enjoying your holidays. See you soon.
Terry

Nick Underhill
64 Pirate Cove
Falmouth TR11 4NB
UK[2]

Friday
Dear Nigel,
I miss you! We're having fun, but I'm thinking about you all the time. We're arriving in Orlando in a few days. Is there a letter waiting for me at my aunt's house? Are you thinking about me too?
My brother talks with an American accent! He sounds very odd. I hope you're having a nice holiday.
Love, Amanda

Mr. Nigel James
24 Ravenswood Road
Truro TR1 2QB
U.K.

[1]A musical play by British composer Andrew Lloyd Webber.

[2]United Kingdom (England, Scotland, Wales, and Northern Ireland).

43
LESSON

BROADWAY
the great white way

Broadway is a major street in New York City. Look at the m

You can see that it starts in the north at Dyckman Street and ends in the south at Battery Park.

Broadway crosses 42nd Street at 7th Avenue. This is Times Square, the theater and film center of the city.

To New Yorkers "Broadway" means the entire theater area—approximately the area between 42nd and 49th Streets from Broadway to 8th Avenue.

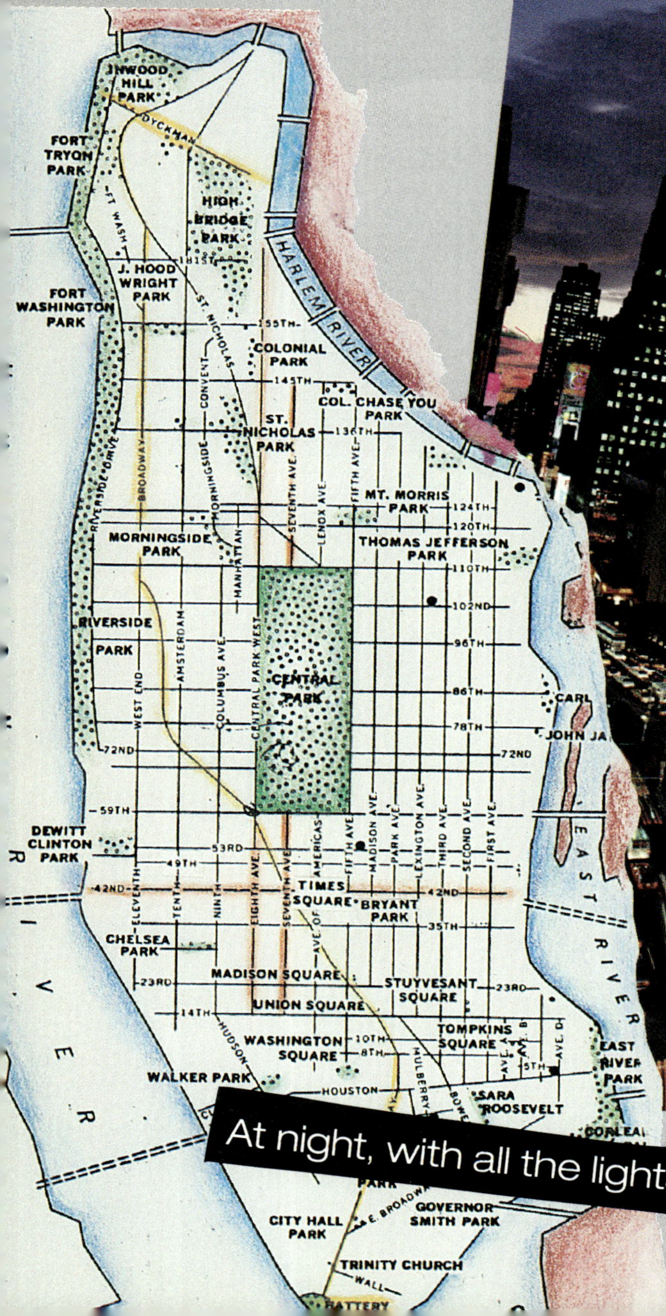

At night, with all the lights on, it is really "The Great White Way"!

Intermission at the Majestic Theatre

Hector: Well, what do you think?

Elaine: I love it! It's an exciting show! The music sounds so beautiful. Michael Crawford is a brilliant actor. He's a perfect phantom. And what a singer! His voice is fabulous! I'm having a wonderful time.

Hector: You really like it.

Elaine: Well, don't you?

Hector: Well . . . no, not really. I agree with you—Michael Crawford is excellent. But the rest is silly.

Elaine: Silly? How can you say "silly"? It's an old French romance . . . a famous story.

Hector: Yes, but it seems silly.

Elaine: What about the music?

Hector: I think the music is too . . . too complicated. One song is very nice, however—"The Music of the Night." But it's really an opera. Everybody sings all the time.

Elaine: What's wrong with that?

Hector: Nothing. I just don't like opera. And our seats are terrible.

Elaine: You're looking at your watch, I see.

Hector: Well . . .

Elaine: Don't worry. It'll be over in about an hour.

Andrew Lloyd Webber

Andrew Lloyd Webber was born in 1948 in London. He is only a young man, but is already a superstar composer with a long list of musical hits.

- *1968* **Joseph and the Amazing Technicolor Dreamcoat**
- *1971* **Jesus Christ Superstar**
- *1976* **Evita**
- *1981* **Cats**
- *1982* **Song & Dance**
- *1984* **Starlight Express**
- *1985* **Requiem**
- *1986* **The Phantom of the Opera**
- *1988* **Aspects of Love**

Michael Crawford

This talented Englishman was born in Salisbury, Wiltshire, in 1942. He is an actor, singer, dancer, and comedian. He makes movies, performs on television, acts in the West End[1] and on Broadway, and sings on record albums. His most famous performance in New York is in the Broadway production of *The Phantom of the Opera*. He has a platinum record in the United Kingdom for The Michael Crawford Album, his first solo record album. He is the recipient of numerous awards, for example, the OBE.[2]

[1]London's theater district.
[2]Officer of the Order of the British Empire.

LESSON 44

Getting in SHAPE

ELAINE: What's the matter, Michelle? You look exhausted.

MICHELLE: I feel awful. I'm not sleeping very well. I'm overweight and I can't stay on a diet.

ELAINE: You sound depressed. Do you get any exercise?

MICHELLE: No, not really. I sit at my desk all day. I'd like to go to a health club, but I can't find the time.

ELAINE: Yes, you can. Everybody can.

MICHELLE: You look great! How much exercise do you get?

ELAINE: A lot. I jog a few times a week and I go to a health club.

MICHELLE: How often do you go?

ELAINE: Three times a week. In fact, I'm going after work today. Why don't you come with me?

MICHELLE: I can't. I have too much work and I'm too tired.

ELAINE: You can come for half an hour. It's just across the street.

MICHELLE: I can't exercise in these clothes!

ELAINE: I have an extra sweatsuit with me. The only problem is shoes.

MICHELLE: I have a pair of sneakers in my desk.

ELAINE: Great! We can go together after work. We can work out together. Then you can decide if you want to join or not.

MICHELLE: I can't join. I don't have the time!

ELAINE: Don't decide now.

This is the schedule of the Upson Downs Health Club.

OPEN:
6 A.M., Monday – Saturday
8 A.M., Sunday

CLOSE:
11 P.M., Monday – Saturday
6 P.M., Sunday

NAUTILUS ROOM:
6 A.M. – 11 P.M., Monday – Saturday
8 A.M. – 6 P.M. Sunday
New members need an instructor with them for their first five workouts. Always call for an appointment.

SWIMMING POOL:
7 A.M. – 10 P.M., Monday – Saturday
8 A.M. – 5 P.M., Sunday

RACQUETBALL COURT:
6:30 A.M. – 10:30 P.M., Monday – Saturday
8:15 A.M. – 5:45 P.M., Sunday
No reservation necessary.

AEROBICS CLASS:
7:00 A.M. M, T*, W, Th, F*, Sat
9:15 A.M. M, W, F, and Sat
10:00 A.M. T, Th
11:00 A.M. Sun
5:30 P.M. M – F
6:30 P.M.* M, T, W
7:00 P.M. T, Th

*Easy aerobics.

Elaine Delgado's Health Club Routine

Elaine Delgado usually goes to her health club three times a week. She sometimes goes at seven o'clock in the morning. She prefers to work out then, but it isn't always easy to wake up early. So she often goes after work. She always begins with a few warm-up exercises and rides a stationary bike for about twenty minutes. Then she works out on the Nautilus equipment. She concentrates on her arms, shoulders, waist, and especially on her thighs and hips. She always finishes with sit-ups and push-ups. Then she swims for a quarter of an hour, spends ten minutes in the sauna, takes a shower, and goes home. She always feels great!

At the health club

LESSON 45

I'd like a little DIET SODA, please

Marta Ortiz lived and worked in California. She was a Spanish teacher in a large high school in Berkeley. She taught there for six years and liked it very much, but she began to get bored with the same people, the same scenery, the same lessons. She thought about her situation and decided to look for a job abroad. She found a British teacher's exchange program and applied for a two-year teaching job at Hamford, a private girls' school near Bristol. The headmistress of Hamford wrote to Marta in April. The job was hers! She was very excited and hoped to leave California in July. She wanted to travel around England for a few months before school began in September. She had a million things to do!

A telephone call

MARTA: Hello?

MICHELLE: Hi, Marta. It's Michelle.

MARTA: Oh, hi, Michelle. How are you?

MICHELLE: Fine, thanks. In fact, I feel great! I lost twenty pounds.

MARTA: You did? Wow! But you weren't heavy, were you?

MICHELLE: Yes, I was. I was a blimp. I gained a lot of weight when I stopped smoking last year.

MARTA: I did, too. And I never lost it. I'd like to lose a few pounds before I go to England.

MICHELLE: That's in a month, isn't it?

MARTA: About five weeks.

MICHELLE: I want to see you before you go. Would you like to come to dinner next Friday?

MARTA: I'd love to. Let me check my date book. Hmm ... Yes, Friday sounds fine.

MICHELLE: Great! Is seven OK?

MARTA: Sure. Is there anything I can bring?

MICHELLE: No. Just yourself.

At Michelle's

When Marta arrived at Michelle's apartment,[1] she gave Michelle a bouquet of beautiful pink flowers. Michelle put them in a vase and offered Marta a drink. "What would you like, some wine, some diet soda . . .? There's some beer in the refrigerator,[2] I think, and a few cans of regular soda. And I think there's a little orange juice."

"I'd like a little diet soda, please. I really want to lose weight," she said. "I only have a month, so there isn't much time."

"Yes, there is," Michelle said. "There's a lot of time. You can lose a lot of weight in four weeks. Would you like to try my diet? There's a copy of it on my desk."

"Sure! It really worked for you."

Dr. Abner's High Energy Diet

Welcome to my quick and easy diet plan. Follow the plan and lose weight fast and easily. Here are some simple rules to follow:

1. Don't eat any sugar or any foods with sugar in them, e.g., cake, ice cream, etc.
2. Drink 8 large glasses of water a day.
3. Don't cook with salt. Do not add any salt to your food.
4. Eat some vegetables every day—at least 2 cups.
5. Don't drink any alcoholic beverages.
6. Get some exercise—at least 20 minutes a day, e.g., aerobics, walking, bicycling, etc.
7. Eat some fish at least 4 times a week. (Eat shellfish—shrimp, lobster, crab, etc.—only twice a week.)
8. Don't drink anything with caffeine in it. Drink decaffeinated beverages.
9. Eat only 2 pieces of fruit a day.
10. Stop eating when you are full.

BREAKFAST

½ cup of yogurt
½ banana or apple
1 slice of toast or 4 ounces of dry cereal
8 ounces of skim milk

LUNCH

3–4 ounces of tuna fish or sliced lowfat ham or 2 hard-boiled eggs
1 medium tomato sliced with lemon juice
1 slice of bread
beverage

DINNER

4–6 ounces of chicken or fish
1 cup (or more) of steamed vegetables
1 slice of bread or ½ cup cooked brown rice
large salad with vinegar and lemon dressing
1 peach, apple, or orange

SNACK

diet soda, cucumbers, tomatoes, radishes, celery, carrots, green peppers

---

British English equivalents
[1]flat
[2]In England and sometimes in the U.S. you will hear "fridge."

46

Is this love at first sight?

LESSON

Marta Ortiz was waiting in line[1] at the post office when she noticed a familiar face. The man was standing in the same line. He was holding a few packages[2] and some letters. He was wearing dark brown pants and a tweed jacket with leather patches on the elbows. There was a pack[3] of cigarettes in his breast pocket. *What a handsome man*, she thought. *Who is he? He looks very familiar, but I can't remember his name. Where did I meet him?* She wanted to say something, but she was afraid. *I can't just start talking to him*, she thought. *What can I say? Can I ask him about the weather? No, I can't. I can't say anything*. She bought some stamps and began to walk to the door. She was walking slowly past him when he turned and looked at her. Their eyes met. She was just beginning to speak to him when he said, "Uh, excuse me, but I'm sure I know you from somewhere. You look very familiar." When he began to speak, she knew something exciting was happening to her. She asked herself, *Is this love at first sight?*

---

[1]You will also hear "on line" in some areas of the United States, especially in New York City. *In line* equals *in a queue* in British English.

[2]Packages are *parcels* in the United Kingdom.

[3]A pack (of cigarettes) is a *packet* in the U.K.

"You look very familiar, too," she replied. He was very tall, with dark brown hair and bright blue eyes. And now his eyes were directly on her.

"You're American," he said.

"Yes, I'm from California," she said.

He looked at her carefully and said, "I was in San Francisco from the second to the twelfth of August. Did we meet there?" He moved closer to Marta and looked at her hopefully.

"No, that's not possible. I came to England on the fifteenth of July," Marta said and then thought, *Maybe I never met him before. Maybe I just want to meet him now*. She didn't know what to say.

"You probably think I'm rude," he said, "but I have to know. My name is Gordon Cameron-Smythe. Does that help?"

Now she understood. "It's a famous name, Mr. Cameron-Smythe. Everyone knows your name. You live in that castle on Walpole Hill, don't you?"

"Well, it isn't a castle, but, yes, yes, I do . . ."

"I saw your picture in the newspaper a week ago. You were attending the races at Ascot."[1]

He was surprised. It was a small photograph. How did she remember?

"I noticed it when I was reading a story to my Spanish class," she replied. "The story was about racehorses, and the newspaper was on my desk. Your picture was on the front page – right in front of me."

"But we still have a mystery, don't we? You saw my photograph in the newspaper. But where did I see you?" he asked. He was confused. They stared at each other for a moment, and then he asked, "Would you like to take a walk?"

"Yes, I would," she answered immediately. "But what about your packages?"

[1]A racetrack near Windsor. A four-day race is held there each year.

"They can wait," he said.

She followed him out of the post office and they walked slowly down Primrose Lane. They didn't talk. Marta knew the answer to the mystery, but she wanted this moment to go on forever. When they reached the corner, Marta stopped. She had to tell him. She turned and looked at him and smiled. "You have a daughter, Cecily. She's my student at Hamford."

"Of course. And a month ago I attended a concert at the school. You were there. I remember. When I saw you, I was thinking . . . Oh, never mind." He looked embarrassed.

"What were you thinking?" she asked. "Tell me."

"But I don't even know your name." They began to walk again.

Then Marta said, "My name is Marta Elena Ortiz. I'm from California. I'm single. And I teach Spanish at the Hamford School on a Teacher's Exchange Program. I like movies, books, and long walks. That's enough about me. What about you?" She looked up at him and smiled.

He smiled too. "Well, Marta. You know my name. I live here in Hamford and I work in Bristol. I'm a widower. I like films[1] too. I also like traveling[2] and gardening. I have no bad habits. Well, only one. I smoke two packets of cigarettes a day."

"What? You smoke?" Marta stopped smiling.

"Yes. Is it a problem?" He looked concerned.

She was gentle but firm. "I stopped smoking almost two years ago . . ."

"I see," he said. "I tried to give it up a year ago, but . . ."

"I can help you," she said, "if you want to . . ."

---

[1]Notice that Marta says *movies* and Gordon says *films*. You will also hear *the cinema* in British English.

[2]You will see *travelling* in British English.

47 LESSON

YES, you can!

Welcome to the first meeting of SmokeStop. My name is Sarah Brown, your group leader. I'm happy you were all able to come here tonight.

Before we begin I have a few announcements. First, you can smoke in this first meeting, but please sit in the back and make sure the window is open. You'll find ashtrays on the table in the corner. Second, you can stay and listen to the first presentation without charge. If you decide to participate, you can pay me in full before you leave tonight or before we begin tomorrow night. The charge is $500. Yes, yes, I know it's expensive. But you'll find that it's worth it. Third, you may not miss one meeting. If you do, you cannot continue the program and we cannot return your money. You will receive a form to sign when you pay the fee. Let me read the form to you. It says, "I will attend every meeting of SmokeStop. If I miss a meeting, I understand that I will not be allowed to finish the program, and my money will not be refunded. However, if I have a doctor's certificate, SmokeStop will return part of the fee. I agree to follow this SmokeStop rule." Are there any questions? No? OK.

Well, let's begin. Let me tell you a little bit about myself. I'm an ex-smoker. Five years ago I was smoking three packs of cigarettes a day. I was miserable. I felt awful. Everything smelled bad. Everything tasted terrible. I couldn't stand it. I tried to stop many times, but I couldn't. I just couldn't. I tried everything—hypnosis, cold turkey, special chewing gum, pills, books, food—but nothing worked. Does that sound familiar to you? I couldn't do it myself. Then a friend told me about SmokeStop. I tried it and it worked. It was as simple as that! One month and I was free. You will be able to do it too. Come to the meetings, do your assignments, and take the program seriously. That's all you need to do.

Now let's watch this videotape. Some very interesting people will tell you how they were able to quit.

INTERVIEWER: How many packs of cigarettes were you smoking a day?

GORDON: Oh, about two packets . . . or three . . .

INTERVIEWER: Did you ever try to quit?

GORDON: Yes, many times. But I couldn't. You see, I was a widower. I had many, many pressures and problems. But I could always sit and relax with a cigarette. I liked to smoke. Once in a while I tried to quit, but I couldn't.

INTERVIEWER: What made you successful this time?

GORDON: My wife, Marta . . . well, she wasn't my wife then . . . suggested SmokeStop. It worked for her. And I decided to try it.

INTERVIEWER: And?

GORDON: Well, it worked. That was a year and a half ago.

INTERVIEWER: Do you notice anything different?

GORDON: Oh, absolutely. Food tastes better. Everything smells better. And I feel better in general.

INTERVIEWER: So you recommend SmokeStop.

GORDON: Oh, yes indeed. I couldn't do it myself. But I could do it with SmokeStop.

I can't do this. It sounds impossible. I won't be able to give it up. I don't have any willpower. And $500! That isn't cheap! I need a cigarette.

I can't hurt myself any more. It's expensive, but I have to quit. This program doesn't sound easy, but it sounds good. I can do it . . . I think.

LESSON 48

It's easier to get tickets to the WORLD SERIES...

On Monday morning Sarah Brown woke up with an earache. It was like an earache she had six months ago. She knew she had to see the doctor. "I'm going to call Dr. Watanabe," she said to Sam, her husband. "It's the same as the earache I had before. I'm sure he's going to prescribe something over the phone—the same antibiotic or something . . ."

Sam asked, "Is it as bad as the earache you had before?"

"I think it's worse, and it's in the other ear," she said.

"Well, Sarah," said Sam. "I'm sure the doctor is going to want you to go to his office."

"I hope not." said Sarah. "I'm very busy at work. It's the busiest time of the year. Maybe I'll call the doctor tomorrow."

"Your health is more important than the office!" said Sam. "Call him!"

Robert Watanabe is an ear, nose, and throat doctor. He has an excellent reputation. In fact, he's one of the best ENT specialists in the country. People come from all over to see him. He has a lot of patients, and it is often difficult to get an appointment. His patients say that it is easier to get tickets to the World Series[1] than to get an appointment with Dr. Watanabe. His waiting room is always crowded, especially on a Monday morning.

[1]An inappropriately named baseball competition between the two best North American teams of the year. It is played in October, and the champions must win four out of seven games.

ANNMARIE: Uh, excuse me, but, uh, could you, uh . . .

SARAH: Yes? Can I . . . uh . . . help you?

ANNMARIE: Well, I . . . uh, this is my first time here, and . . . well, I wonder . . .

SARAH: You want to know about the doctor.

ANNMARIE: Yes. I'm sure he's good. But I hate to go to doctors. So I'm a bit nervous.

SARAH: I'm more nervous than you are, and I know Dr. Watanabe very well. He's the best ear, nose, and throat doctor around.

ANNMARIE: Really? Is he . . . uh . . . nice?

SARAH: Oh, yes. He's the nicest, kindest man in the world.

ANNMARIE: I hope he's nicer than his nurse.

SARAH: Oh, don't pay attention to her. She's always grumpy. She's usually less grumpy in the afternoon. But she's OK.

ANNMARIE: Is Dr. Watanabe . . . uh . . . old?

SARAH: Old? Well, let's say he's older than you and younger than me. By the way, what's your problem?

ANNMARIE: I have a sinus condition. I have a horrible headache. It was bad on Saturday, worse on Sunday. But today it's the worst.

NURSE: Mrs. Brown?

SARAH: Yes! Don't worry, dear. It's going to be fine.

ANNMARIE: Uh, excuse me, but, uh, could you, uh . . .

NURSE: This is your first time here, right?

ANNMARIE: Yes. I'm visiting my aunt and uncle. They're patients here.

NURSE: I see. Well, we're going to do a few tests before you see the doctor. Please step on the scales. Let's see . . . you weigh 119 pounds.

ANNMARIE: That's eight stone seven.

NURSE: I beg your pardon?

ANNMARIE: In England we say our weight in stone. A stone is fourteen pounds.

NURSE: What about height?

ANNMARIE: Oh, that's the same as here. I'm five feet two.

NURSE: Don't you use the metric system?

ANNMARIE: Yes. In supermarkets and other shops for weighing and measuring things.

NURSE: I see. Well, on to the EKG.

ANNMARIE: The what?

NURSE: The electrocardiogram. It measures the pattern of your heartbeats.

ANNMARIE: Oh, right. We say ECG.

NURSE: We say both. But this is very interesting.

ANNMARIE: Pardon me?

NURSE: Well, American English is very different from British English.

ANNMARIE: Right. American English isn't the same as English!

LESSON 49 I'll be WAITING for you

Norma Franklin went to the drugstore to get some medicine. She had a prescription from her doctor for an antibiotic and a special nasal spray. She felt awful. She had a horrible headache, her nose was stuffy, and she was dizzy. She wanted to take the medicine as soon as possible because she had an important appointment in the afternoon. Unfortunately, there was a long line at the prescription counter. *Everybody in town is sick, I think*, said Norma to herself. *And I can hardly stand up.* She went up to the young pharmacist and asked, "Excuse me, but how long is it going to take? I'm going to be late for an appointment."

"It's going to be just a few more minutes," he replied. "There are a few people ahead of you. Two of our pharmacists are home sick today. I'm sorry."

Drat! Norma thought. *I'm going to call Fred. I hope he's still at home.* She found a pay phone and called Fred. She said, "Look, I'm just waiting for a prescription. I'm going to be leaving here in a few minutes. Where will you be waiting?" she asked.

"I'll be waiting for you on the northeast corner of Maple and Green," he replied. "We'll be meeting the clients at the Tivoli Restaurant." Then he said, "You sound awful, Norma. Will you be feeling OK later? We're going to be working very hard. Are you up to it?"

"I'll be feeling better as soon as I take the medicine. See you soon."

She went back to the counter and waited, and waited, and waited. There were a lot of people there, more than before. Finally, after about twenty minutes, she said to the young pharmacist, "Look, I really have to go. Can you tell me when my medicine will be ready?"

"Sure. What's your name again?" he asked.

"Franklin, Norma Franklin."

He looked under the counter and said, "Oh, it's right here. It was ready twenty minutes ago. I called your name, but you weren't here."

"Drat! I was making a phone call," she said. "Oh, well. I'm just going to be late. How much is it?"

"That'll be $46."

"What? For an antibiotic and a nasal spray? I can't believe it!" She was totally surprised at the amount.

"Will you be paying cash?" he asked.

"No, here's a credit card," she said, sighing.

The young pharmacist filled out the credit slip and gave it to Norma. She signed it and ran out of the drugstore. *I'm already twenty minutes late*, she thought as she ran down the street. *I hope he's still there. This isn't going to be a good day!*

Milton Brooks is home after a hard day at the drugstore. He worked quite a few hours today and he's exhausted. He can't go to bed yet because he wants to unwind. So he's eating a TV dinner and watching a popular talk show.

Don't go away, folks. We'll be right back after this word from our sponsor, GERM-BLAST.

Flu season is here and poor Caroline feels awful. She has a terrible sore throat, her eyes are watering, and she can't breathe.

Teddy is sneezing and coughing. His body aches and he can't breathe. He also has a fever.

They're both busy people. They need a medicine that will provide instant relief. There are quite a few cold remedies available, but there's only one effective kind—GERM-BLAST. It's better than aspirin, better than cough medicine, better than nasal sprays. Take GERM-BLAST and you'll feel fine for twelve hours. You'll be sleeping better! You'll be breathing better! You'll be feeling better! Believe me! Take GERM-BLAST. You'll thank me.

I recommend GERM-BLAST for fast, effective relief.

GERM-BLAST is a miracle. I feel like a new person. There's only one cold remedy for me—GERM-BLAST!

LESSON 50

You HAVE to HAVE one

About three weeks ago Milton Brooks saw a woman in the drugstore where he worked. She was picking up a prescription for cough medicine. She often came into the drugstore, and he knew her name because it was on the prescription. He thought she was attractive, with an intelligent face and a nice smile, and he wanted to ask her for a date. But he just didn't know how. And there were always a lot of people around. Then a few days later he was in the bookstore next to the drugstore. So was she—examining language books. She didn't recognize him. He wanted to talk to her but he didn't know how to begin. Then he thought of a way. He began to examine the language books too.

"Excuse me, you're Sandy Keller, aren't you?" he asked.

"Oh, hi. You're . . . oh, yes, you're the pharmacist in the drugstore next door," she said.

Milton thought, *Oh, great! She recognized me.* He said, "Yes, I'm Milton Brooks. So . . . what language are you studying?" he asked her. He was a little nervous and hoped that he didn't sound rude.

"Oh, I'm not studying any language. My friend is going to Greece and I'm looking for a going-away gift for her. How about you?"

It was so easy. She was so nice. "Spanish. I have to learn Spanish," he answered. He wasn't nervous any more.

"Really? You have to?" she smiled.

"Well, I have some family in Venezuela. I'd like to go there next summer to visit and I only know a few words of Spanish. Uh, do you speak any other languages?"

"I speak Spanish and a little French," she replied.

"Well, I can't speak either one," he said.

They talked for a while and agreed to meet for a drink at P. J. Clarkson's at six o'clock that evening. Milton was thrilled. He couldn't wait! He thought, *I hope it turns into dinner!*

The next day . . .

Milton is having lunch with his college friend Nikos, a photographer.

Milton: Let me ask you something, Nikos . . . Do you have an American Express card?

Nikos: No, I don't.

Milton: Neither do I.

Nikos: But I have a Diner's Club card, VISA, MasterCard, and a couple of department store cards. How about you?

Milton: I don't have any. I always pay cash. But . . .

Nikos: What? You mean you carry a lot of cash around? That's asking for trouble. You *must* get a credit card. How can you live without one?

Milton: I don't know. I just never applied for one. And last night I got myself in a lot of trouble because I didn't have one.

Nikos: What happened?

Milton: I went to dinner with this woman. I really wanted to impress her. But when the check came, I didn't have enough cash to pay.

Nikos: Who paid?

Milton: Well, *she* had to. I'm sure she'll never go out with me again.

Nikos: Listen, pal, you have to get a credit card. You just have to get one.

Milton: Which is the best one?

Nikos: Well, with VISA or MasterCard you don't have to pay the entire balance every month.

Milton: Yes, but they charge you a very high interest rate on the unpaid balance, don't they?

Nikos: Well, yes . . .

Milton: Well, after last night, I know I have to do it. I'll get the American Express® Card.

Nikos: OK, so will I.

Milton: Maybe I'll get the Gold Card.

Nikos: Milt, don't overdo it.

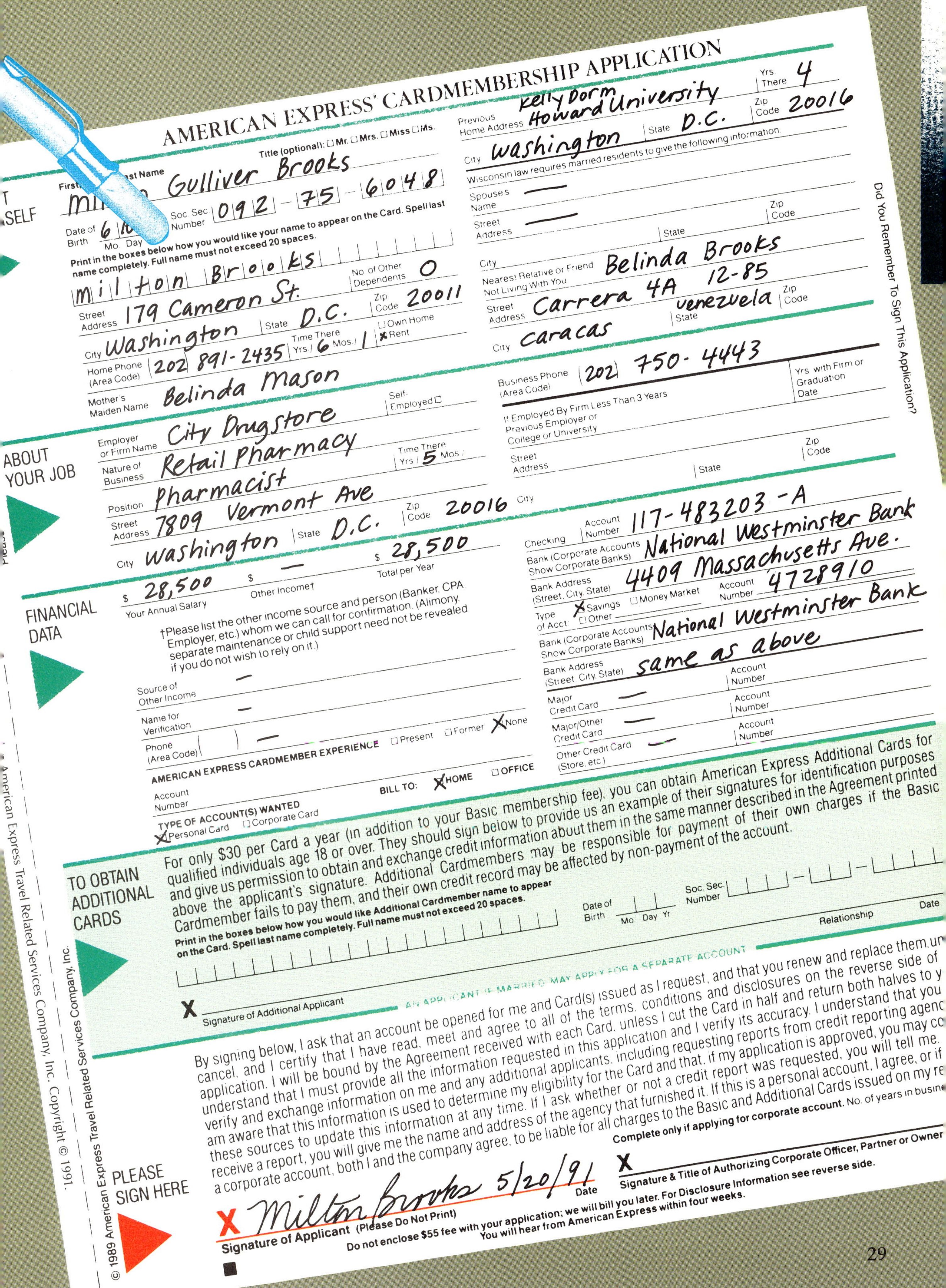

AMERICAN EXPRESS® CARDMEMBERSHIP APPLICATION

T
SELF

Title (optional): ☐ Mr. ☐ Mrs. ☐ Miss ☐ Ms.

First ... Last Name: Mi... Gulliver Brooks

Date of Birth: 6 / 1... (Mo. Day)

Soc. Sec. Number: 092 – 75 – 6048

Print in the boxes below how you would like your name to appear on the Card. Spell last name completely. Full name must not exceed 20 spaces.

Milton Brooks

No. of Other Dependents: 0

Street Address: 179 Cameron St.

Zip Code: 20011

City: Washington — State: D.C.

Time There: Yrs. 6 Mos. 1 — ☐ Own Home ☒ Rent

Home Phone (Area Code): 202 891-2435

Mother's Maiden Name: Belinda Mason

Previous Home Address: Kelly Dorm Howard University — Yrs. There: 4

City: Washington — State: D.C. — Zip Code: 20016

Wisconsin law requires married residents to give the following information.

Spouse's Name: —

Street Address: — State — Zip Code

City

Nearest Relative or Friend Not Living With You: Belinda Brooks

Street Address: Carrera 4A 12-85

State: Venezuela — Zip Code

City: Caracas

ABOUT YOUR JOB

Employer or Firm Name: City Drugstore — Self-Employed ☐

Nature of Business: Retail Pharmacy — Time There: Yrs. 5 Mos.

Position: Pharmacist

Street Address: 7809 Vermont Ave — Zip Code: 20016

City: Washington — State: D.C.

Business Phone (Area Code): 202 750-4443 — Yrs. with Firm or Graduation Date

If Employed By Firm Less Than 3 Years Previous Employer or College or University

Street Address — State — Zip Code

City

FINANCIAL DATA

Your Annual Salary: $ 28,500 — Other Income† $ — — Total per Year: $ 28,500

†Please list the other income source and person (Banker, CPA, Employer, etc.) whom we can call for confirmation. (Alimony, separate maintenance or child support need not be revealed if you do not wish to rely on it.)

Source of Other Income: —

Name for Verification: —

Phone (Area Code): —

Checking Account Number: 117-483203-A

Bank (Corporate Accounts Show Corporate Banks): National Westminster Bank

Bank Address (Street, City, State): 4409 Massachusetts Ave.

Type of Acct: ☒ Savings ☐ Money Market ☐ Other — Account Number: 472891O

Bank (Corporate Accounts Show Corporate Banks): National Westminster Bank

Bank Address (Street, City, State): same as above — Account Number

Major Credit Card: — Account Number

Major/Other Credit Card: — Account Number

Other Credit Card (Store, etc.): — Account Number

AMERICAN EXPRESS CARDMEMBER EXPERIENCE ☐ Present ☐ Former ☒ None

Account Number — BILL TO: ☒ HOME ☐ OFFICE

TYPE OF ACCOUNT(S) WANTED ☒ Personal Card ☐ Corporate Card

Did You Remember To Sign This Application?

TO OBTAIN ADDITIONAL CARDS

For only $30 per Card a year (in addition to your Basic membership fee), you can obtain American Express Additional Cards for qualified individuals age 18 or over. They should sign below to provide us an example of their signatures for identification purposes and give us permission to obtain and exchange credit information about them in the same manner described in the Agreement printed above the applicant's signature. Additional Cardmembers may be responsible for payment of their own charges if the Basic Cardmember fails to pay them, and their own credit record may be affected by non-payment of the account.

Print in the boxes below how you would like Additional Cardmember name to appear on the Card. Spell last name completely. Full name must not exceed 20 spaces.

Date of Birth (Mo. Day Yr) — Soc. Sec. Number — Relationship — Date

AN APPLICANT IF MARRIED MAY APPLY FOR A SEPARATE ACCOUNT

X Signature of Additional Applicant

By signing below, I ask that an account be opened for me and Card(s) issued as I request, and that you renew and replace them un... cancel, and I certify that I have read, meet and agree to all of the terms, conditions and disclosures on the reverse side of application. I will be bound by the Agreement received with each Card, unless I cut the Card in half and return both halves to y... understand that I must provide all the information requested in this application and I verify its accuracy. I understand that you verify and exchange information on me and any additional applicants, including requesting reports from credit reporting agenc... am aware that this information is used to determine my eligibility for the Card and that, if my application is approved, you may co... these sources to update this information at any time. If I ask whether or not a credit report was requested, you will tell me. receive a report, you will give me the name and address of the agency that furnished it. If this is a personal account, I agree, or if a corporate account, both I and the company agree, to be liable for all charges to the Basic and Additional Cards issued on my re...

PLEASE SIGN HERE

X Milton Brooks — 5/20/91 Date

Signature of Applicant (Please Do Not Print)

Complete only if applying for corporate account. No. of years in busin...

X Signature & Title of Authorizing Corporate Officer, Partner or Owner

Do not enclose $55 fee with your application; we will bill you later. For Disclosure Information see reverse side. You will hear from American Express within four weeks.

LESSON 51

THEY'VE BEEN TOGETHER FOR 65 YEARS

Tomorrow night Nikos Kanelous is leaving for Greece to attend his grandparents' anniversary party. He can't leave until the evening because he has to take a final exam in the morning. He's getting a master's degree[1] in cinematography. He's meeting his sisters at the airport and they are all going to Athens together.

Nikos and his two sisters live in the United States. Their parents died many years ago, but they still feel very close to their family in Greece. Nikos hasn't been there for five years, and he's looking forward to seeing everybody—his brother Spyros, cousins, aunt and uncles, nieces and nephews. He's especially looking forward to seeing his cousin Kostas, an architect married to an Englishwoman, Kathleen. Kostas and Kathleen have visited Nikos in the United States many times, and they have often invited Nikos to visit them in Athens.

Nikos is showing pictures of his family to his friend Milton. "Here's my cousin Kostas, and this is his wife, Kathleen. Here's their daughter, Irene.

"Here are my grandparents. I talk to them by phone regularly, but I haven't talked to them since January. They've been together for sixty-five years and they're still happy!

"This is my Aunt Daphne on my mother's side and her third husband. She's a psychologist, but she hasn't worked for years. She has eight children.

"These are my great uncles, Yiorgos and Yannis, that's George and John in English.

"And this is my parents' house. Well, I guess it's my house now. Spyros and his family live there now, but someday . . ."

---

[1]The master's degree is higher than the bachelor's degree. The doctorate is higher than the master's. All of these are university-level degrees.

At the anniversary party . . .

Excuse me, but haven't we met before? I'm sure I've seen you some . . .

Yes, we *have* met. At Kathleen and Kostas's wedding. I'm Louise Norris, Kathy's sister. You're Nikos, aren't . . .?

Yes. It was at the wedding in London. Have you seen a lot of Ath . . .?

Well, I've been here before, of course . . .

Look . . . I've got a few days left . . . Maybe we could . . .

Why, yes. I'd be happy . . .

Great! Have you visited the Acropolis and the Parth . . .

Yes, but I'd like to go aga . . .

How about tomorrow morn . . .

That would be wonder . . .

Where are you stay . . .

At my brother-in-law's hou . . .

Really? So am I. I've just arrived today. I didn't know you were th . . .

I didn't know eith . . .

At the airport in Athens . . .

I wish I could stay.

I do too. I've had the best week of my life.

So have I. It's been great.

You've shown me some wonderful places. And your family has been so nice to me.

I don't have your address and phone number.

You haven't asked me.

I'm asking now.

Here it is. I've put it in this letter.

Letter?

Read it on the plane.

OK. But when can we see each other again?

I don't know. But I do know one thing. I have never been as happy as I am now.

Neither have I. Have you made plans for next summer?

No, I haven't.

Either I'm going to England or you're coming to the United States. How about it?

I have three weeks' holiday . . .

Then come to the States.

I have to think about it. But I'll write and let you know.

You have to come . . .

Yes, I know.

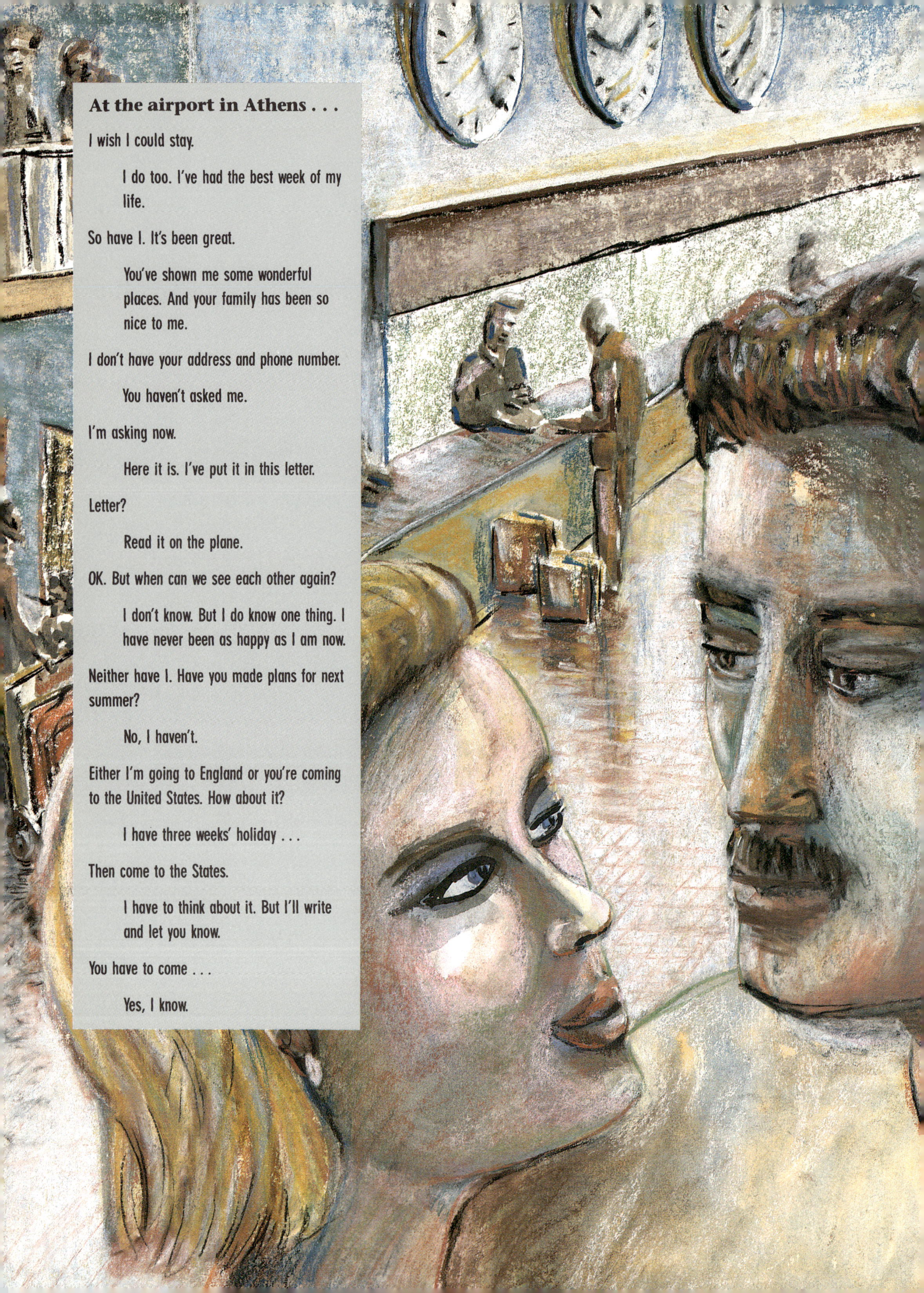

LESSON 52

I had the BEST TIME I've ever had in my whole life!

Dear Niko:[1]

My trip back to England was awful. I was sitting next to a woman with a young boy who cried and screamed the whole way. The woman was very nice and I felt sorry for her. But I wanted to strangle that child! The flight attendants gave him some games but he wasn't interested! He wanted my bracelet, but I wouldn't give it to him, so he screamed even louder. It was impossible to sleep, so I spent the whole time thinking about the time you and I spent together.

Did you read the note I gave you before you left Greece? Perhaps I said too much. I hope it didn't embarrass you. It's easier to write about my feelings than to talk about them.

I've been here for two weeks and I haven't done anything except think about you and Greece. I had the best time I've ever had in my whole life. I've thought about next summer, and of course I want to come to see you. I've traveled a lot—all over Europe—but I've never been to the States. I've never flown across the Atlantic. I think this is the perfect time to do it. I've got a three-week holiday in August. Would that be convenient for you? Please let me know right away so I can begin to make some plans.

I can't wait to hear from you!

Love,

Louise

[1]The final *s* is usually dropped from Greek names in direct address.

LOUISE: Come in, Peter.

PETER: Louise, it's wonderful to see you. I've missed you.

LOUISE: It's nice to see you too, Peter. Do sit down. How have you been?

PETER: Very well. But tell me about your trip. How was it?

LOUISE: Peter, I had the best time I've ever had in my whole life.

PETER: I see. How . . . uh . . . wonderful.

LOUISE: My brother-in-law's family was so hospitable. And the party was super.

PETER: Well, that's very . . . nice . . .

LOUISE: Would you like something to drink? Some tea? Or maybe a drink?

PETER: No, I don't think so. Are you having one?

LOUISE: Yes, a glass of red wine.

PETER: Well, I'll have one too.

A few minutes later . . .

53 GET ON with your LIFE

LESSON

Mrs. Ashfield: What is the matter with you, Peter? You've been behaving very strangely for weeks.

Peter: Oh, it's nothing, Grandmother.

Mrs. Ashfield: Don't tell me it's nothing, Peter. I can see for myself.

Peter: I've had some problems. I've been rather unhappy lately.

Mrs. Ashfield: Yes, and you haven't been eating properly.

Peter: I haven't been very hungry.

Mrs. Ashfield: And you haven't been seeing your friends.

Peter: I haven't felt like going out.

Mrs. Ashfield: I know all about it. It's that woman Louise, isn't it?

Peter: Well, yes.

Mrs. Ashfield: Another man, isn't it?

Peter: Uh, yes.

Mrs. Ashfield: Pull yourself together, Peter. She isn't worth it. You'll find someone else. Look at me! I've had many difficulties in my life. And I have survived very well. Don't you think so?

Peter: Well, yes, Grandmother, but . . .

Mrs. Ashfield: Don't "but" me, Peter. Get on with your life.

Peter: Well, all right.

Mrs. Ashfield: How is your book coming along?

Peter: I haven't written a word since March.

Mrs. Ashfield: Since March? That's terrible! When is your deadline?

Peter: December.

Mrs. Ashfield: Well, get cracking!

After his conversation with his grandmother, Peter tried to get back to his writing. His book is about older people who have kept their careers going even into their eighties and nineties. His grandmother, Mrs. Ashfield, is one of his subjects.

PORTRAITS*

Claudio Arrau

This internationally famous pianist was born in Chile in 1903 and has been playing professionally since 1908. After World War II broke out, Claudio and his German wife, Ruth Schneider, left Germany and immigrated to the United

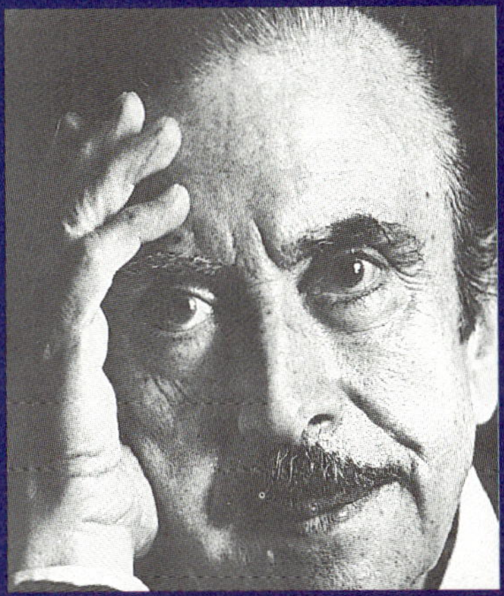

States. In the past, this extraordinary pianist gave 140 concerts each year, but now he has reduced his performances to approximately 90. He has decided to play for as long as possible and has said, "... I get strength from performing."

Constance Ashfield

This outspoken British author was born in 1900 in Chesterfield. Mrs. Ashfield has been writing books for children since 1920. She wrote her last book, *Auntie Jackie and the Dinosaur* in 1980 when she was 80 years old. Mrs. Ashfield says, "I have been writing stories for over sixty years. And I am going to continue for sixty more years. I haven't finished yet!"

George Burns

This nonagenarian entertainer was born Nathan Birnbaum in 1896 in New York. He has been an actor, dancer, singer, and comedian since 1903. And he's been making people laugh for three quarters of a century. He has been married only once—to actress Gracie Allen, his partner in comedy until her death in 1964 after thirty-eight years of marriage. His trademark is a cigar. Someone once asked him, "Has your doctor ever told you to stop smoking?" George answered, "Every doctor has. And they've all died."

*At the time this lesson was written, all these famous older people were alive.

Alexandar Solzhenitsyn

Born in 1918 in the Soviet Union, this novelist has been living and writing in Vermont since 1974. He is most famous for his novel *One Day in the Life of Ivan Denisovich* (1962). He has received many awards, including the Nobel Prize for Literature in 1970.

Martha Graham

This energetic dancer and choreographer was born in Pittsburgh, Pennsylvania, in 1895. She has been dancing since 1920, when she made her professional debut. She has received many awards, among them the Presidential Medal of Freedom which she accepted in 1976. Miss Graham retired in 1970 but has been directing her dance company since then. She has been carefully recording on videotape all of the dances she has created. This is for future generations of dancers and dance lovers.

Robertson Davies

This prolific Canadian novelist has been an actor, playwright, journalist, and newspaper editor. His first book, *Tempest-Tost*, appeared in 1951. In the 1980s he produced an extraordinary work, *The Deptford Trilogy*. He has been serving as Master of Toronto's Massey College for many years.

54

LESSON

I haven't got a lot of time

Peter Ashfield and his wife, Joyce Crowe, have been married for two years. They met each other when Peter went to New Zealand to research a story. It was love at first sight. They got married one month after they met.

Joyce, who has kept her name for professional reasons, is from Hamilton, a charming city on the west coast of North Island. She is a travel writer for a local newspaper, and she has written many articles for magazines and newspapers abroad. She has already written two travel books, one called *The Land of the Kiwi*[1] and the other one called *The Art of the Maori*.[2] She was working on her second book when she met Peter. He was doing research for an article on longevity and wanted to interview some centenarians in New Zealand. He went to the local newspaper in Hamilton and happened to meet Joyce. They have been together ever since.

Joyce and Peter have decided to write a book about why some people live longer than others. They have been interviewing older people in New Zealand, England, and the United States. They have already met more than 85 men and women over 100, but they haven't finished yet! Next month they are going to the Soviet Union for three months and then they are going to China.

Peter and Joyce have been using a small tape recorder to record the interviews. One of the people they have talked to is Carl Petrie. He says he is more than 100 years old, but he isn't sure exactly how much more. His oldest great-grandson, Thomas Petrie, was also present at the interview.

[1]the native bird of New Zealand
[2]the Polynesians who migrated to New Zealand approximately 1200–1400 A.D. before the first Europeans arrived

Joyce: Mr. Petrie, we've been looking forward to meeting you.

Thomas: He's been looking forward to meeting you too. I hope this won't take too long. My great-grandfather is very tired.

Carl: No, I'm not, Tommy. Let me talk. Well, young lady. What would you like to know?

Joyce: Mr. Petrie, tell us about yourself—your early days.

Thomas: He came to New Zealand when . . .

Carl: I can talk for myself! I came to New Zealand when I was a small boy. We came from England. My father was a sheep farmer, and I followed in his footsteps. I saved my money, started a family, and bought some land. I've become very rich. But I started as a farmer, and I'm still a farmer.

Peter: You have a very large family, Mr. Petrie, don't you?

Thomas: Oh, it's very large. My great-grandfather . . .

Carl: Tommy, will you please let me speak? I have a very large family, and it's still growing. Well, you see, I've been married three times. Eleven children are still living. I have twenty-six grandchildren and forty great-grandchildren—Tommy here is one. He's a nice boy, but he talks too much!

Joyce: I see . . . Well, why do you think you've lived so long, Mr. Petrie? Have you done anything special?

Thomas: Oh, he's always taken care of himself.

Carl: And I'm about to take care of you, Thomas. *Be quiet!*

Thomas: Sorry.

Carl: Well, as I was saying . . . What was I saying? Oh, yes. I haven't done anything special. I've been exercising and eating right all my life. I've always eaten a lot of good New Zealand lamb. I still do. And I've been drinking spirits[1] all my life. I'm about 110 years old, and I still feel fine. I don't know why.

Joyce: Is there anything you haven't done yet?

Carl: What do you mean, young lady?

Joyce: Well, have you done everything you've wanted to do in your life?

Carl: Oh, yes, I've already done everything. I've already made a fortune, flown in a jet, gone around the world. Well, there's one thing I haven't done yet.

Peter: What's that, Mr. Petrie?

Carl: I haven't seen my first great-great-grandchild yet. So Thomas, hurry up and get married. I haven't got a lot of time left.

American English equivalent
[1]alcoholic beverages

LESSON 55

She's the BEST RUNNER I've ever seen

Julio Alonso, a columnist for *World Sport* magazine, has just returned to the United States from New Zealand. He was there doing research for an article on young female New Zealand athletes. While he was there, he stayed with his friends, Peter Ashfield and Joyce Crowe. They live in a small country home near Wellington. Now Julio is in his apartment in Chicago. He is sitting at his new state-of-the-art IBM word processor writing an article about a young New Zealand runner.

OK, fans of long-distance running. I'm giving you some information. I'm giving it to you because it's important—it's the most important news I've ever told you. In a few years you'll tell me, Julio, you were right! So listen to me. Take me seriously. I'm telling you the truth.

Anne Hannam, a young New Zealand runner, is simply the best newcomer I've ever seen. And I predict that she'll be the star of the next summer Olympics. She's the most flexible cross-country runner I've ever met. She has endurance, concentration, and a great determination to win.

Anne Hannam grew up in the North Island city of Lower Hutt, near the capital of Wellington. Her mother died when she was 16. It was the most terrible thing that ever happened to her. But her strict father expected excellence from his children. And Anne became an "A" student and an excellent violinist. In 1984 she joined a runners' club in Auckland, not for the exercise, but to meet new friends. By the summer and fall of 1988, Anne set some new world records.

July 31	**Alaska 10-K Classic**	**32:40**
September 3	**Colorado 10-K**	**33:09**
September 18	**Fair Lakes 10-K**	**32:14**
September 24	**Virginia 10-Miler**	**54:40**
October 10	**Tufts 10-K for Women**	**31:38**
October 22	**Bowling Green Classic 10-K**	**31:33**
October 29	**Tulsa Run 15-K**	**48:13**

Now she's ready for the Olympics!

Anne is happily married to a chef for New Zealand Air. However, she has to spend a lot of time without her husband in the beautiful high Colorado mountains. There she trains by running about 120 miles a week at an altitude of 5,400 feet. It is probably the most difficult training she has ever done! But she wants to be the best long-distance runner in the world. And she has to defeat women like Grete Waitz of Norway, Joan Benoit of the United States, Rosa Mota of Portugal . . .

Julio stopped writing and reread the beginning of his story. He thought, *Maybe this isn't the worst story I've ever written, but it's not one of my best. It doesn't say anything about Anne Hannam. I have to start over.*

He decided to take a break. He walked around his living room and thought, *Maybe I'll redecorate the apartment.* He looked around the room. *What an ugly old green rug! In fact, it's the ugliest rug I've ever seen. I need a new one. And look at this horrible shabby old chair. I can't live like this anymore. I need a decorator! Maybe when my apartment looks good, I'll be able to write.*

56

I've Decided to Get My Apartment Redecorated

LESSON

Julio Alonso decided to get his apartment redecorated. He told his friend Paul, "I've lived here for fifteen years. And I've had the same furniture. I need a change." He didn't know any decorators and he didn't want to do the work himself. So he looked in the Yellow Pages. Here's what he found.

The Complete Decorator
Residential · Commercial · Institutional

clubs · banks · stores · lobbies · offices · schools · showrooms · institutions · restaurants · corporations · hotels · homes · apartments

We do a careful, painless, complete job. Satisfaction guaranteed. Call 334-7000 for a free consultation.

AMERICAN DESIGNERS
Architectural interiors, space planning, and design

A new dimension in design and decorating services for business and home

Color consultation	Windows	Paint and
Fine furniture	Interior decoration	wallpaper
Carpentry	Slipcovers	Wall decor
Draperies	Carpets	Mirrors

We are famous for honesty, cleanliness, perfection.
And we always get the job done quickly and carefully.
Call us at: 445-0349

The Japanese Designer

Shoji screens
Tatami rooms
Gardens
Carpentry
Complete design and fulfillment

Call: 421-0098

Julio had no idea how to choose a designer. So he asked his friend Paul's wife to recommend a decorator. She gave him the name of somebody with a good reputation.

Donna: Well, you need a lot of work here, Mr. Alonso.

Julio: I know, Ms. Delacorte. That's why I called you.

Donna: I'd like to meet Mrs. Alonso.

Julio: I'm a widower. I live alone.

Donna: I see. Hmm . . . well . . . Uh, let me look around for a moment. Oh, yes. The space is very nice. It's light and sunny. But look! Your drapes are too heavy and they're hung poorly. I'll have drapes made from a lighter fabric. Hmm. Yes. I'm sure I can work quickly and efficiently on this apartment.

Julio: What about the cost?

Donna: Don't worry, Julio. May I call you Julio?

Julio: Sure, Donna.

Donna: Don't worry about the cost. I'm sure I can get this done inexpensively. I'll give you an estimate before I do anything.

Julio: Good.
Donna: Well, we need to get the walls painted and we have to have this horrible carpet removed. In fact, this furniture has aged badly.
Julio: I'd like a Turkish carpet—maybe a Kayseri . . .
Donna: You really know your Oriental carpets, don't you, Julio?
Julio: Well, I've spent a lot of time in Turkey. I've traveled a lot.
Donna: Yes, I've noticed all your wonderful artifacts. Let's look at the kitchen.
Julio: It needs work.
Donna: Yes, of course. We'll have new cabinets built. And you need a microwave oven and a dishwasher.
Julio: And I want to have the den made into an office.
Donna: Excellent. You know, Julio, I think we'll work very well together.
Julio: I think so too.

57 LESSON

I'll Have Done my HOMEWORK *by then!*

Nancy Kawabata is in the loan office of the Englewood Bank. She's talking to Barry Fein, the loan officer, about borrowing some money. He has just asked her to tell him a little bit about herself.

"Well, Mr. Fein, my name is Nancy Kawabata. I've been working as a secretary since I was eighteen years old. I'm twenty-four years old now, and I would like to start my own business. I think I'm an excellent interior decorator, and occasionally I help my friends redecorate their apartments on a free-lance basis. I have a six-year plan. First I should get a degree in interior design. By August I will have saved enough money to go back to school. I plan to work while I'm studying, so I'll have enough to live on – you know, for rent, food, and so on. I figure by 1994 I will have received my interior design license."

Barry asked her when she needed the loan.

"Oh, not for a while. You see, when I get my license, I should work for a few years. I should get some experience before I start my business. So I plan to work with my mother's friend, Mrs. Donna Delacorte Alonso, for two years. She has an interior decorating firm. Have you heard of her company, The Perfect Place? You should call her if you need to redecorate. Anyhow, by 1996 I will have worked for two years as a decorator."

The loan officer was very impressed with Nancy, but he couldn't give her a loan at that time – he wanted to talk to her about it in more detail.

"Ms. Kawabata, I'm very impressed with your plan. Unfortunately, I cannot lend you the money because you don't need it now. But you should come back when you finish school and get your interior decorator's license."

He was very impressed at what she said to him next.

"Oh, I understand that. But you see, I always plan ahead. That's why I'm here now. I'll come back to see you in 1996. And I'll have done my homework by then. I'll have received my license, researched the market, located adequate office space, priced office equipment, chosen a name, designed business cards and stationery, and written a business plan including a detailed budget of expenses for the first year. So you see, sir, you should definitely give me the business loan then."

Barry Fein had to smile. And after Nancy Kawabata left his office, he burst out laughing. He thought, *I wonder what I will have accomplished by 1996 . . .*

* * *

Barry went home that evening and talked to his wife about his day at the bank.

He said, "Well, then this young woman came in. I asked her to tell me about herself. She opened her mouth and closed it ten minutes later. It was amazing. She told me her six-year plan for going into business for herself."

Karen asked, "What else did you talk about?"

"We didn't talk," he said. "*She* talked."

Then Karen asked, "By the way, Barry, did you speak to Jack Kilmer at the bank today?"

"Yes. He says not to worry. They've had our mortgage application for over a month. He says we'll get an answer by next Friday." Barry thought for a few seconds. Then he said, "But I think we won't have gotten an answer by then. It usually takes about six weeks."

"You should insist on an answer, Barry," she said. "You work at the bank."

"That's true. But we don't get any special privileges," he said.

"You should," she said.

"You're right," he agreed, "we should."

58 LESSON

Why don't you talk it over?

Eddie and Janice Matthews have been putting off making a decision for a long time. But they have finally made up their minds. They are going to buy a house. They have lived in the same apartment for ten years. It is a beautiful apartment, but it's hard to bring up two young children in a three-room apartment. They looked up northern New Jersey real estate agencies in the newspaper and called one up. They made an appointment with a sales representative, Paula Grand, at Walker Realtors.

Paula: Would you like to tell me what you're looking for?

Janice: It should be roomy — at least four bedrooms — and it should have some land. It should have an acre of land if possible.

Eddie: And close to the city. We'll be driving there every day.

Janice: It should be near a shopping center and an elementary school.

Paula: Well, the children can go to school by bus.

Janice: No, I'd like to drive them.

Paula: I see. May I ask what you want to spend?

Eddie: Not more than $200,000.

Paula: What about town houses? Would you consider them?

Janice: It depends . . .

Paula: Why don't you look these over? They're descriptions of houses in your price range. Pick out a few that you like and we can see them at your convenience.

Janice: Oh, this one is beautiful. It's perfect.

Eddie: May I see that? Hmm. Janice, it's out of our price range.

Paula: Well, why don't you talk it over? Perhaps you could go higher . . .

Eddie: Well, maybe we could.

Here are some of the houses they looked at.

Price: $260,000
Location: Jamestown
Land: ½ acre
Age: new
Design: Colonial
Stories[1] 2
Basement: full, finished
First: living room, dining room, bedroom, kitchen, full bath, powder room
Second: three bedrooms, den, full bath
Taxes: approx. $3,800
Comments: near schools, transportation, beautiful landscaping, air conditioned

Price: $170,000
Location: Plainsburg
Land: 1 acre
Age: built 1897
Design: Tudor
Stories: 2
Basement: none
First: living room, dining room, den, kitchen, family room, powder room
Second: three bedrooms, bath
Taxes: approx. $3,100
Comments: needs work, fine woodwork, good buy, excellent possibilities

Price: $157,000
Location: Joville
Land: Corner lot 75′ × 100′
Age: built 1970
Design: Ranch
Stories: 1
Basement: none
First: living room, kitchen, dining room, powder room, 4 bedrooms, 1 bath
Second: —
Taxes: approx. $2,900
Comments: excellent location, newly renovated

Price: $209,000
Location Fort Hill
Land: 2 acres
Age: built 1962
Design: Victorian
Stories: 2 plus attic
Basement: full, unfinished
First: living room, kitchen, dining room, bedroom, powder room
Second: 3 bedrooms, 2 baths
Taxes: approx. $4,000
Comments: garage and small barn on lot, finished attic

[1]Singular is *story*. In British English, *storey–storeys*.

LESSON

I recently heard from

Buying a House: Daydream or Nightmare?

by Michael Schaeffer

I recently heard from my old friend Norman. He called to tell me that he has decided to buy a house. That's very interesting because I'm thinking about buying a house too. Sometimes I sit alone at my desk before work and I draw houses. I think I'll call a real estate agent next week so I can begin to look for a house. Or maybe I'll wait. I'm just not sure.

Norman is a dentist. He wants to have his office in his house. So the house has to be large with two separate entrances. Norman told me that he hasn't been himself lately. He thinks about houses morning, noon, and night. He looks at houses with his fiancée in different towns every week. He looks in the real estate section of the newspaper every morning. He looks at the prime lending rate every week. Sometimes he hears about houses for sale from his friends at work. He follows every lead. A few months ago he saw a house he liked a lot. He went back to see it a week later. The owner had already sold it. Another time he saw a beautiful house. It was perfect—the right size, close to the city, near public transportation. It had a huge yard, and it even had a swimming pool. It looked like the house where he was born. His fiancée loved it too, and the price was right. He made an offer the next morning so he would not lose the house. But then he had the house inspected. Poor Norman! The house had termites, asbestos in the basement, leaking water pipes, and a broken hot water heater. He was very disappointed. His fiancée wanted to give up. Norman wanted to try again. He's been looking for a year. I wish him luck.

IT ISN'T EASY TO BUY A HOUSE. FIRST OF ALL, YOU LOOK FOR HOUSES YOU CAN AFFORD. BUT YOUR REAL ESTATE AGENT WANTS YOU TO LOOK AT HOUSES YOU CAN'T AFFORD. YOU GO OVER YOUR FINANCES AGAIN AND AGAIN. YOU WANT TO BE SURE YOU HAVE ENOUGH MONEY FOR A DOWN PAYMENT- USUALLY 15% OF THE PURCHASE PRICE. YOU RUN INTO PROBLEMS. YOU HOPE YOU CAN FIND A BANK THAT WILL GIVE YOU A MORTGAGE. AND YOU WANT TO BE SURE YOU EARN ENOUGH MONEY TO PAY THE MORTGAGE EACH MONTH. YOU DON'T WANT TO RUN OUT OF MONEY.
THEN THERE ARE OTHER PROBLEMS ... TAKE ME, FOR EXAMPLE. I'VE NEVER HAD TO LOOK AFTER A HOUSE. I DON'T KNOW ABOUT HEATING SYSTEMS AND ELECTRICAL THINGS. I DON'T KNOW THE DIFFERENCE BETWEEN A FURNACE AND A HOT WATER HEATER. I CAN'T FIX THINGS. SO I'M A LITTLE NERVOUS ABOUT BUYING A HOUSE. BUT EVERYBODY DOES IT. AND I GUESS I WILL HAVE TO LEARN.

Six months later . . .

I found it! It's great. It isn't huge, but it's big enough. It's close to public transportation and a shopping mall. I went back to see it five times, and I made an offer. I've had it inspected, and I've already filled out the mortgage application. I hope I don't run into any problems. I hope to get it. I can't live without it!

RESIDENTIAL LOAN APPLICATION

Amount $125,000 Interest Rate 10.5% Number of Months 180 Monthly Payment $1,250

Property Address: Street 1023 Ponce de Leon Avenue, N.E. City Atlanta

County Fulton State Georgia Zip 30301

Purpose of Loan: Purchase ✓ Construction _____ Refinance _____ Other (Explain) _____

Title will be held in what name(s):

Borrower:

Name: Norman White Age: 30 School: years

Present Address: Number of years: 7 Own _____ Rent ✓

Street: 1570 Emmet St. City, State & Zip: Charlottesville, Virginia 22901

Former Address: (if less than 2 years at present address)

Street: N/A City, State & Zip:

Years at former address:

Marital Status: Married _____ Unmarried (single, divorced, widowed) ✓ Separated _____

Name and Address of Employer: Norman White, DDS
15 Ellewood St. Charlottesville, VA 22901

Years employed in this profession 5 Years on this job 4 Self-Employed ✓

Position/Title: Doctor of Dentistry Type of business: Dental Office

Social Security Number: 117-28-2033 Home Phone: 804-295-1905 Business Phone: 804-971-4520

GROSS MONTHLY INCOME

Base income $5,835
Overtime: 0
Bonuses: 0
Commissions: 0
TOTAL: $5,835

MONTHLY HOUSING EXPENSES

	PRESENT	PROPOSED
Rent	$1,550	
Real Estate Tax	—	$1250
Mortgage	—	$1,250
Hazard Insurance	—	$60
Utilities	$65	$90
TOTAL	$1,615	$1,650

ASSETS:

Description	Cash
personal Property	$23,000
Georgia Bank, Savings Account #678 21702	$10,000
IRA	$2,120

LIABILITIES:

Creditor	Unpaid Balance
MasterCard	$300
Macy's Department Store	$860
Car Loan from Security Credit Co.	$4,300
School Loans from Peachtree Savings + Loan	$8,800

*N/A = not applicable

YES, you will! NO, I won't!

LESSON

"What's the matter, Jean? You seem preoccupied with something," said Marlo. Jean was looking nervously at the TV set. "Is it the calculus exam tomorrow?" Marlo asked.

"Not really," said Jean. She picked up *TV Program Week* and began to study it. "It's just—well, do you ever watch *Inheritance*? It's on in five minutes."

"You mean that silly soap opera?" asked Marlo. "I've never seen it. I never watch soap operas. Don't tell me you do."

"Uh, well, I watch it sometimes. Well, I mean I never watch TV—only movies and news programs, but I sometimes watch *Inheritance* because, well, it's very entertaining. I like to watch it after a hard day at work. It helps me unwind." Jean turned on the TV and switched to Channel 14. She turned down the volume.

"It's too silly to watch, I think," said Marlo. "But for heaven's sake, if you want to see it, turn it on. I'll watch anything once. I should be studying for the exam . . . Oh, well, why not? What's it about?"

"Well," said Jean. "It's about four generations of the Wonderstone family. They're very rich and . . ."

"And I suppose everything happens to them—murder, divorce, betrayal, infidelity, kidnapping—the usual things," said Marlo.

"Well, of course. Otherwise it wouldn't be fun!"

"OK," said Marlo. "It sounds ridiculous enough to watch—once!"

"Great," said Jean, turning up the volume. There was a commercial on. A famous actress was talking about a perfume named after her.

"Listen, while that horrible commercial's on," said Marlo, "tell me about the fascinating characters in this silly story."

Inheritance

the cast of characters

Marlon Bingham Wonderstone is the 85-year-old head of the Wonderstone family of Atlanta, Georgia. He is the founder of Wonderstone Industries, a multimillion-dollar company that manufacturers mobile homes. He has married twice since his divorce from Carolyn.

Carolyn Fitzpatrick Wonderstone Granger Hayes is 79 and a widow. She married twice after her divorce from Marlon. Both her second and third husbands died in strange accidents. She and Marlon are the parents of two children.

Sylvia Wonderstone Yamamoto, 50, is the daughter of Marlon and Carolyn, and the wife of Japanese industrialist Kenji Yamamoto. They are childless.

Marlon Wonderstone, Jr., is the 62-year-old son of Marlon and Carolyn and brother of Sylvia. He is now president of Wonderstone Industries. He is weak and does everything his father tells him to do in his personal as well as his business life. Everyone calls him Junior.

Alice Crawford Wonderstone, 59, was one of the three beautiful Crawford girls of Newport and Boca Raton. She is still beautiful. She and Marlon, Jr., have two children.

Marlon Wonderstone III is the 38-year-old vice president of Wonderstone Industries. He lost an arm in the Vietnam War and is still bitter.

Portia Wonderstone, 25, is Marlon Senior's favorite grandchild, perhaps because she is as strong-willed as him. When she was 17, she ran off and married the rock star Cary Glitter. That marriage lasted less than six months. She is now in love with the family dentist.

Norman White, 30, is a struggling young dentist.

Mimi Wonderstone is 23 and Marlon Senior's fourth wife. She was a dog walker before she married the multimillionaire.

And now, back to our story . . .

Marlon, Sr.: You will marry Ronald Southern Connor.

Portia: I will not!

Marlon, Sr.: Yes, you will. You're perfect for each other.

Portia: I won't marry him, Grandfather. I don't love him. I love Norman!

Marlon, Sr.: My dear, listen to reason. Ronald will inherit his father's estate. And Ronald is a United States senator. He's influential enough to be president some day. You can be first lady.

Portia: I won't do it! I will marry Norman White. I love him.

Marlon, Sr.: That dentist? You won't marry him. You're too good for him.

Portia: Too good? Never! I'm not good enough for him.

Marlon, Sr.: My dear, that man will never be welcome in this house.

Portia: I don't care.

Marlon, Sr.: Then I have no alternative. I'm cutting off your inheritance. Think about it. You've never worked a day in your life. You don't know how to get a job—you have no job skills. And without money you'll starve.

Portia: I will? Hmm . . . On second thought . . . Maybe you're right. I've never worked . . . Norman will never earn enough money . . . First lady? Hmm . . . I wonder what Ronald is doing tonight?

LESSON

The engagement was announced...

Who painted the portrait of you?
It was painted by Groth.

The engagement of Portia Margaret Wonderstone, the daughter of Mr. and Mrs. Marlon Wonderstone, Jr., to United States Senator Ronald Southern Connor, was announced yesterday at a reception at the home of Senator Connor's parents, Mr. and Mrs. William Southern Connor. Ms. Wonderstone is a granddaughter of the late Marlon Wonderstone, founder of Wonderstone Industries.

Wedding

Portia Margaret Wonderstone, the daughter of Mr. and Mrs. Marlon Wonderstone, Jr., of New York, Atlanta, and Palm Beach, Florida, and a granddaughter of the late Marlon Wonderstone, founder of Wonderstone Industries, was married yesterday to Senator Ronald Southern Connor, son of Mr. and Mrs. William Southern Connor of Atlanta, Dallas, and Palm Beach. The ceremony was performed by the Reverend Andrew F. Wilson at Grace Church-on-the-Green in Atlanta. The reception was held at the Ivy League Club in Atlanta.

Who wrote the article about the wedding? It was written by Cora Carton.

When Ronald Southern Connor was a boy, he made a promise to himself. "I will be president of the United States." When he said this, he was told by most people, "Isn't that cute, Ronnie." But he was told by his father, "You can do anything you want to do. You can be anything you want to be."

Ronald did very well in school. He got good grades and was accepted at Harvard. After he graduated from Harvard Law School, he practiced law for a few years.

When he was twenty-eight, he was elected mayor of Springfield. That was eighteen years ago. Since then he has worked hard on his climb toward the presidency of the United States. When he was thirty-two, he was nominated by his political party to run for the United States Senate and was elected by a large majority. He was reelected once and has served almost two full terms.

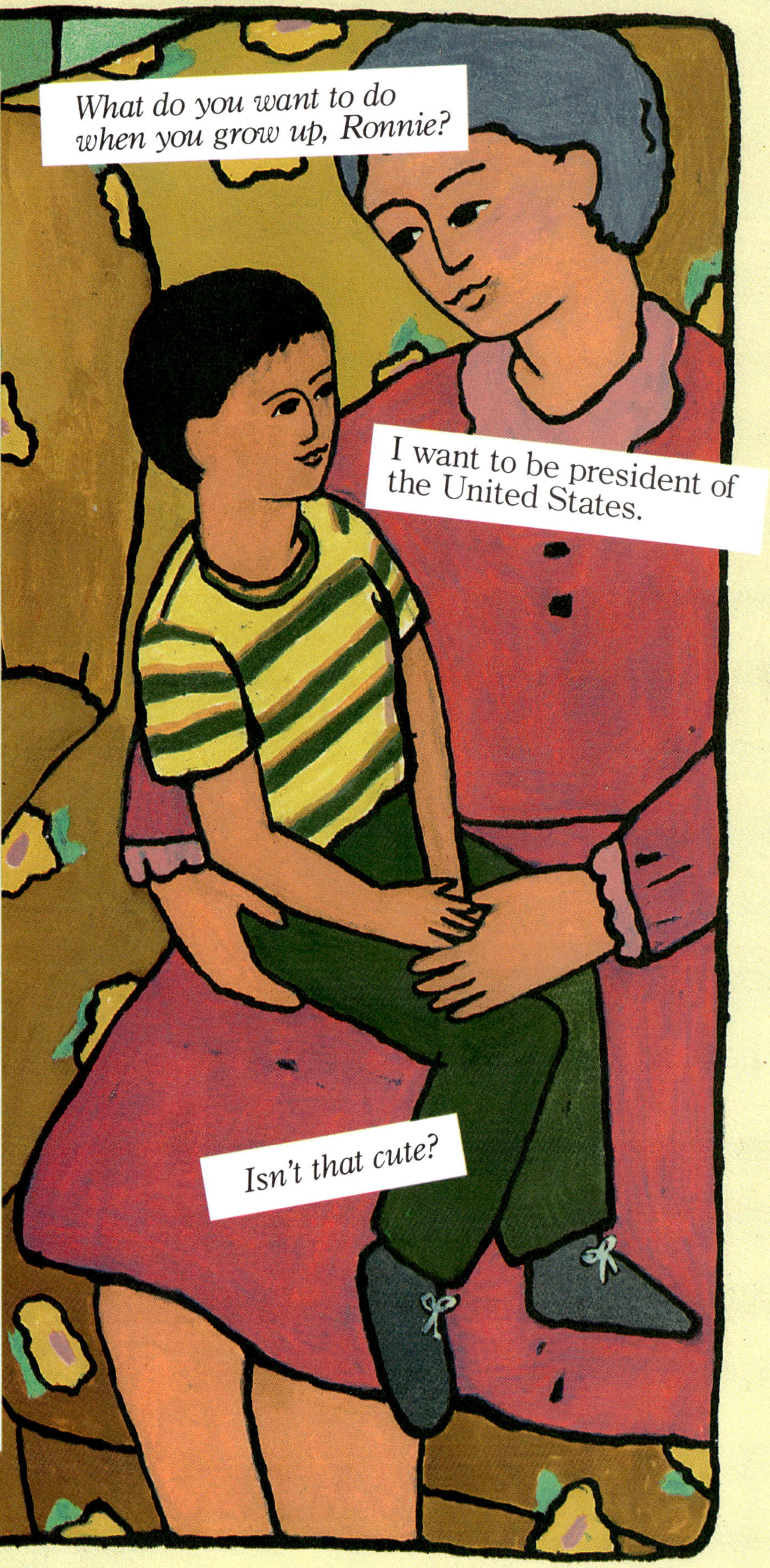

Now he is seeking the nomination for the presidency. He is determined to make it.

Hello. My name is Ronald Southern Connor. This is my wife, Portia, and our children, Ronald, Jr., Peter, Jane, and Marsha. We have always lived in this beautiful state. Our children were all born here. As you know, I was elected to the United States Senate twelve years ago. Before that I was mayor of Springfield. During that time I was asked by the President to serve on a special committee to study drug abuse. I was awarded a medal for my work with inner-city kids. When I was elected to Congress, I made a few promises. Do you remember? Now that my time as a senator is ending, let me review what was accomplished in our state during my twelve years as your senator.

62 LESSON

THE ELECTORAL COLLEGE–
It isn't understood by most people!

Good evening, ladies and gentlemen, and welcome to *Just the Facts*, a production of the Public Broadcasting Company. My name is Jeffrey Brockman, and I am your host this evening. *Just the Facts* is a program of news and information on all subjects—it is designed for everyone. Three topics are presented each hour. Tonight our first topic is the electoral college, the controversial system that elects the president and the vice president of the United States. The electoral college isn't understood by most people, but it is an interesting topic this year—the year that Senator Ronald Southern Connor received the majority of the vote of the people—that is, the popular vote—but lost the presidential election. How did it happen? Stay tuned. We'll return after these messages from PBC.

After you see *Just the Facts*, you'll want to stay tuned to *Science for the Nineties*, an update of the latest developments and discoveries in the world of science. That's at nine o'clock.

At ten o'clock we bring you Part 21 of Tolstoy's *War and Peace*. Now here's Miranda Calvin, vice president and general manager of Channel 67.

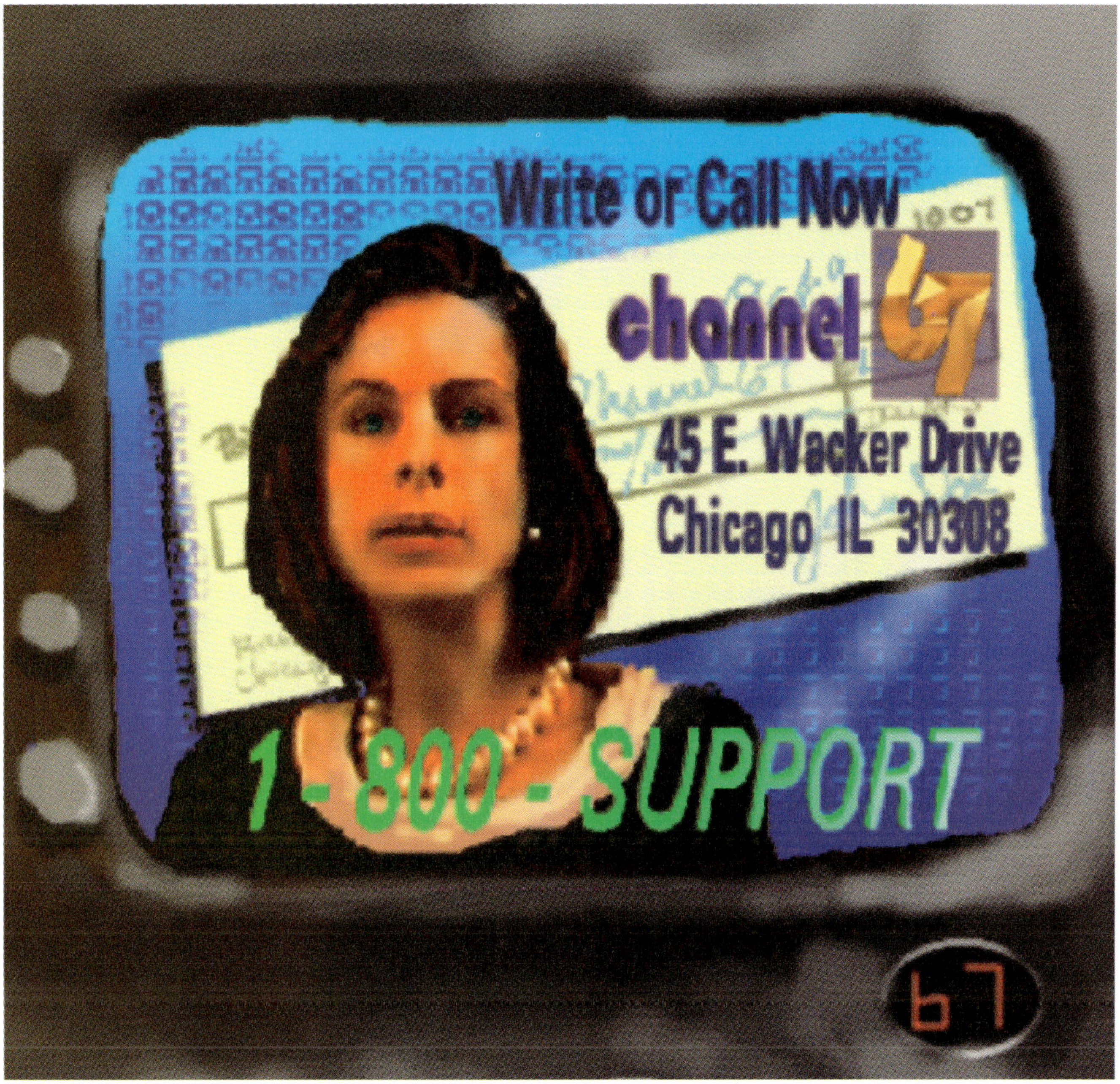

Hello, again. Before we return to *Just the Facts*, I want to talk to you for a moment. I only need a few minutes of your time. As you know, public television needs your help. Channel 67 is supported by your generous donations. So please help us again. Before you watch *Just the Facts*, one of the wonderful public television broadcasts, call us at 445-9000 and make a pledge. Or after you watch *Just the Facts*, take out your checkbook and send us a donation. The address is on your screen now.

After we receive your donation of $35, our magazine, *Patterns*, will be sent to you each month. For a donation of $50, this beautiful Channel 67 umbrella will be sent to you.

Or would you like this beautiful Channel 67 Limoges platter? It will be sent to you after we receive your donation of $100 or more. We are supported by you. Wonderful programs are brought to you because of your generosity. Channel 67 needs your help. Thank you. Now back to our program.

Hello, again. Did you know that the president and the vice president of the United States are not elected by the direct vote of the people? Did you know that three presidents were not elected by the popular vote but by the electoral college? They were John Quincy Adams in 1824, Rutherford B. Hayes in 1876, and Benjamin Harrison in 1888. And did you know that John F. Kennedy almost lost the popular vote to Richard M. Nixon in 1960? Out of a total of 68,300,000 votes, JFK won the popular vote by only 118,550 votes!

Each state is given a number of electoral votes. These are based on the number of its senators and its representatives in Congress. Each state has two senators. The number of representatives is determined by the population of the state. A census is taken every ten years and an apportionment is made after each census. The total number of representatives is fixed at 435; there are three electors from the District of Columbia; and there are 100 senators. So there are 538 electoral votes. A candidate must get 270 electoral votes to win the election. A person who receives the majority of the popular vote in a state is given *all* of that state's electoral votes.

Now how can a candidate win the popular vote but lose the election? Let's take two states as an example. Look at this chart:

Electoral votes		**Popular votes**	
		Candidate A	**Candidate B**
California	**47**	**5,876,212**	**4,982,716**
Wisconsin	**11**	**989,607**	**2,809,522**
TOTAL		**6,865,819**	**7,792,238**

Candidate A has won the popular vote in California and is given 47 electoral votes. Candidate B has won the popular vote in Wisconsin and is given 11 electoral votes. Candidate A gets 81% of the electoral vote but only 47% of the popular vote. Nevertheless, Candidate A is declared president.

Is this fair? What do you think? We want to hear from you.

63

I'll TRY to get used to it!

LESSON

Jamie Fletcher is a producer of documentary films. His company, JF Films, has produced many documentaries for public television. He and his staff are now working on a proposal for a new one. Cal Barnett is the fund raiser. He sells ideas to large corporations, which give money to support the projects. Roy Shapiro sells the projects to public television. Jamie, Cal, and Roy are used to working together. Although they formed JF Films more than twenty years ago, they are still good friends and they work well together. Barbara Engle is the creative director. She's been with JF Films for twelve years. She's used to working long hard hours with the three men, and she enjoys her job. Colleen Murray is Barbara's assistant. Although she's been with JF Films for only a month, she's been doing a good job. George Goodman is a new employee too. He's a film director. This will be his first project with JF Films. There are other employees at this meeting. Some of them are hearing about the project for the first time.

the temples at Angkor Wat

Mont-Saint-Michel

the pyramids at Uxmal and Chichén Itzá

the Toronto Tower

Jamie: OK, everyone, settle down. We have a lot of brainstorming to do here. And unless we write an intelligent, impressive proposal, we won't get the money for this project.

Cal: Do we have any leads?

Roy: Sure we do. The usual ones. But we're going to need millions for this one.

Barbara: I'm not used to working with such a big budget. But I'll try to get used to it!

Jamie: OK. This will be a thirteen-part TV program. We're starting with thirteen parts, but there are hundreds of possibilities for more.

George: Why is that?

Jamie: Don't interrupt me until I finish. For now the program is being called *Wonders, Old and New*. Each episode will focus on a wonder of the ancient or modern world.

Colleen: You mean natural wonders like waterfalls and mountains?

Jamie: No, I mean wonders created by human beings.

George: Unless I'm mistaken, it's nothing new!

Jamie: It *is* new! Everybody is used to seeing travelogs about each of these

the Kremlin

the Dome of the Rock

Chartres

the Great Wall of China

the Colosseum

the Buddha in Kamakura

the Taj Mahal

the Alhambra near Granada

the pyramids at Giza

Stonehenge

Sistine Chapel

the Escorial

the Acropolis

the Empire State Building

the Statue of Liberty

monuments, statues, places . . . But in ours, we're going back in time. Each episode will take place during the creation of the wonder, or a few years after.

Colleen: So there will be a storyline, a drama.

Jamie: Right! We'll show the monument being built, the statue being sculpted, the wall being erected, and so on.

Barbara: It sounds like a *son et lumière*[1] show, only with actors, not just lights and voices.

Jamie: Exactly! But don't interrupt me. We need writers, actors . . .

Barbara: Unless I'm wrong, this will take years to produce.

Jamie: Right! We could go on forever! Now here's an incomplete list of "wonders." Although there are more than twenty on the list, I want you each to choose only thirteen of them. Then we can begin. You can also add a wonder that is not on my list.

Jamie: Can you think of any more?

Barbara: You bet I can!

Colleen: Not me. I've never heard of some of them!

the Roman Forum

the Eiffel Tower

Machu Picchu

Mount Rushmore

the Leaning Tower of Pisa

the Sphinx

the Sears Tower

[1]A special way of showing a historical event at a historical site using lights, music, and recorded or live narration.

LESSON 44

I used to be a WIMP

Best boy: Super Success commercial, take one!

Narrator: Colleen Murray has just started a new job. She's really happy about it because it's exactly the right job for her. She's also very surprised and pleased with herself. You see, Colleen Murray used to be a wimp.

Colleen: Yes, I used to be a wimp. I . . . uh . . .

Director: Cut! I don't believe this! Her lines haven't been learned yet. And she hasn't been made up. What's going on around here?

Colleen: Sorry, Mr. Brickman. I can't say "wimp." It isn't right.

Director: But we've rehearsed this a thousand times.

Colleen: Look, I know the lines, but, well, I don't like the word "wimp."

Director: But that's the idea. You used to be a wimp before you took the Super Success course.

Colleen: Well, yes, but . . .

Director: Let's go.

Best boy: Super Success commercial, take two.

Director: And action.

Narrator: Colleen Murray has just started a new job. She's really happy about it because it's exactly the right job for her. She's also very surprised and pleased with herself. You see, Colleen Murray used to be a wimp.

Colleen: Yes, I used to be a wimp. I used to be afraid to talk to people. I never had any dates. And I used to have only boring, dead-end jobs.

Narrator: Then Colleen heard about Super Success, the weekend seminar that gives you all the tools you need for super success in business, in love, in life.

Colleen: That's right. I've gained self-knowledge, confidence, awareness of my strengths and weaknesses, independence, ambition, energy, vitality . . . I've been offered hundreds of interesting jobs. And now I have the best job in the world. I'm the assistant to the creative director of a major documentary production company.

Narrator: Colleen has many friends, goes to wonderful restaurants, travels to exotic places . . .

Colleen: I used to stay home a lot. But my new job has given me the opportunity to travel. In fact, I've just come back from China and Japan.

Narrator: You, too, can have all the opportunities Colleen had. In just one Super Success weekend seminar, here's what you will be able to do:

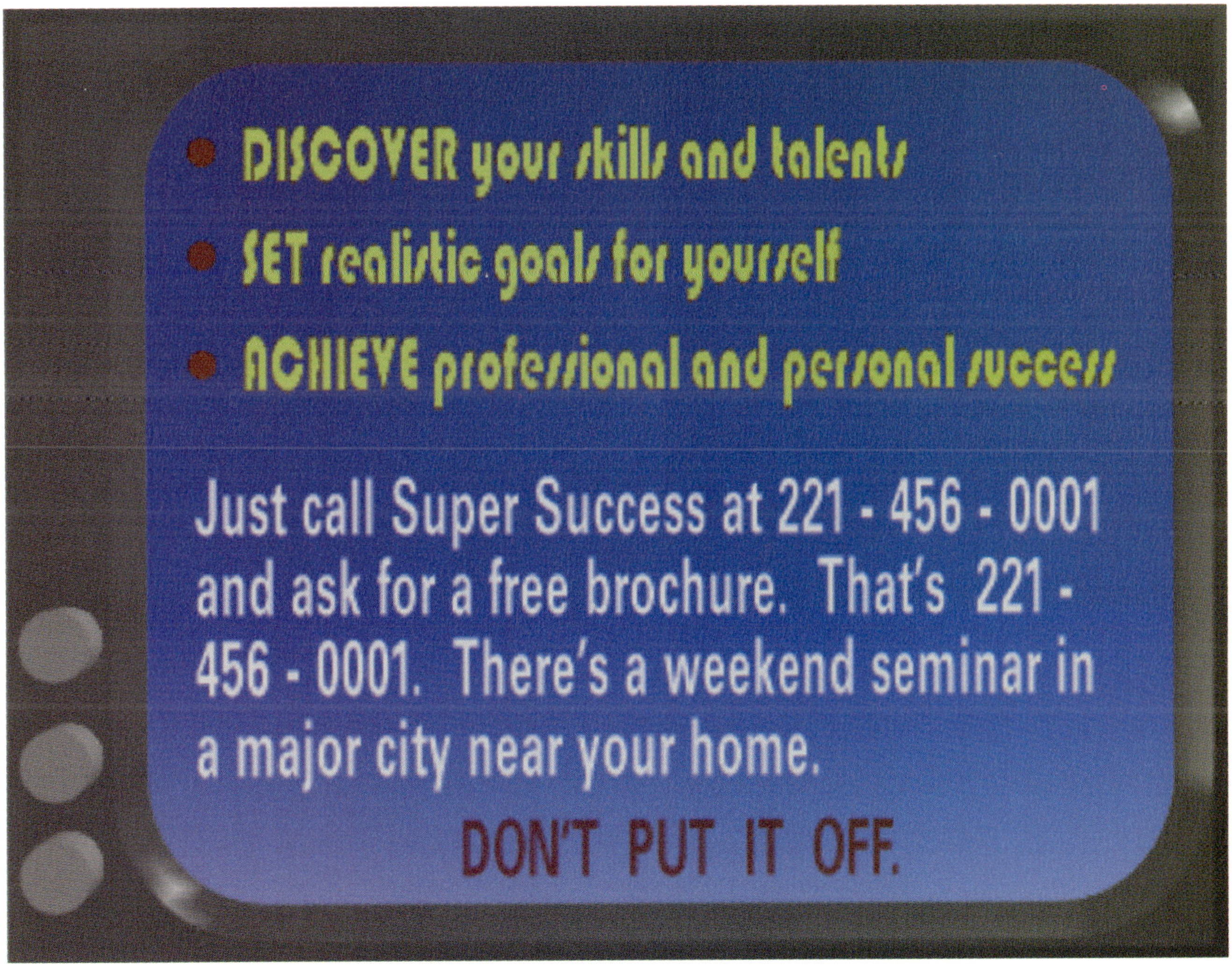

Director: Cut! That was OK. Let's try it again.

Colleen: Wait a minute. Mr. Brickman, may I talk to you for a minute?

Director: Yes, sure.

After the conversation Mr. Brickman said to the company, "We're going to change one of Colleen's lines. Instead of 'I used to be a wimp,' Colleen is going to say, 'I used to be shy and self-conscious.' "

It looks as if the Super Success seminar worked for Colleen. Here's what she said to Mr. Brickman: "Unless you change the word 'wimp,' I refuse to sign a release form."

LESSON 15

I had always been shy and self-conscious until...

SUPER SUCCESS

The powerful two-day weekend seminar

David McDonald

By the time I took the Super Success seminar, I had already been fired from four jobs. I had never found work that I really liked. And I hadn't found anyone who really liked me. I started my own business six months after I had taken the seminar. It's a computer program design business. By the time the first year was over, I had already planned to open two more offices. Now I am a success! I have a fascinating business, I am my own boss, I make a lot of money, and I have prestige.

Sandra Carpenter

I had always wanted to be a lawyer, but I was afraid to speak in public. I had always been shy. But I knew that I had to become more outgoing. The summer after I had graduated from college and was waiting to go to law school, I decided to do something about my problem. I attended the Super Success seminar. Well, it worked. Now I always speak in front of large groups and I enjoy it. I am a successful trial lawyer.

BILL HUDLEY

I participated in a Super Success seminar about six years ago. I had just lost my fiancée when I went to the seminar. I was lonely and unable to meet people. My friends tried to help me, but nobody had succeeded. It was a terrible time for me. A friend told me about Super Success. A week after the seminar, I met my future wife. We have been married for five years. I have never been so happy!

Barbara Camera

I had always been shy and self-conscious. Now I am outgoing and secure. I have wonderful friends, a good job, and lots of hobbies and interests. I had never thought about acting, but now I am in a theater group. Thanks to Super Success!

Professor Stanley Goldman

I had been a loser all my life. I hadn't been able to succeed at anything. I had gotten average grades in school and I had never had a good job. I had always tried—at least I thought so—but nothing great had ever happened to me. I had always been interested in economics, but I didn't know what to do with it. My parents had always tried to encourage me to get a university degree, but I never listened to them. Then I heard about Super Success. It was a miracle! After the weekend, I applied to a college and I was accepted very quickly. Well, that was years ago. I now have a Ph.D. degree in Economics and I am a professor at a prestigious university. I recommend Super Success to everyone.

Super Success seminars are held the third weekend of every month. Call 212-777-7000 to find out about the next seminar in your city.

COLIN: I received a brochure for some peculiar seminar—Super Success. Do you know anything about it?

BARBARA: Sure. I took the seminar. It was wonderful.

COLIN: It sounds like a gimmick to me.

BARBARA: No, it isn't a gimmick. It really worked for me.

COLIN: What do you mean "worked"?

BARBARA: Well, look at the brochure.

COLIN: Good heavens! That's you!

BARBARA: Yes. Before the end of the seminar I had agreed to let them use my picture. That is if I felt that I had become successful. And I did! Become successful.

COLIN: How do you know?

BARBARA: Well, before we went to the seminar, we had received a homework assignment. We had to write down twenty goals we wanted to achieve in the next five years. At the seminar we learned how to achieve the goals.

COLIN: What did you write?

BARBARA: Oh, I wrote things like "have an apartment in the city and a house in the country, have an exciting job, earn a lot of money, drive a Porsche, marry a wonderful man." Those are five.

COLIN: How many of the twenty goals did you achieve?

BARBARA: Eighteen, but I still have a year to go.

COLIN: That's great, but I'm still skeptical.[1]

---

[1]*Skeptical* is spelled *sceptical* in the U.K.

LESSON 66

He had been appearing regularly

Colin Colethorpe is an interesting guy. He's from England but has been living in the United States for about twenty years. He's a very successful actor, but the love of his life is his acting school, The Actor's Place, which he opened ten years ago. Before that, he had been appearing regularly in movies,[1] in the theater, and on television.[2] You probably wouldn't recognize him. He's a character actor and his specialty[3] is accents. So he looks and sounds completely different in every role he plays. Before his school became profitable, he had been performing a few roles in some TV movies. But that was only to help pay the rent. Now he is earning a good living from the school, and he rarely performs.

British English equivalents
[1]*films*
[2]*the telly* (informal)
[3]*speciality*

Maybe you've seen him in one or two roles:

As the Adventurer in the TV mini-series *The Borneo Brigade.*

As Dr. Watson in the TV production of the Sherlock Holmes story *The Redheaded League.*

As Captain Bligh in the TV production of *Mutiny on the Bounty.*

As the Mad Hatter in the children's TV movie *Alice in Wonderland.*

One of the most interesting courses at The Actor's Place is called "Auditions and How to Survive Them." Colin had been planning to teach the course even before the school opened. Young actors had to be aware that there are hundreds of actors for every role. So he required all of his students to take the course. He still does. Colin often thinks back to one particular audition. It wasn't his first, but it was awful. It was for a part in a musical play called *Let's Sing, Let's Dance*. He had been practicing for weeks before he went to the audition. He had been rehearsing at a dance studio for hours every day and taking singing lessons. He had a script and had been practicing a soliloquy for a month. He had been working so hard because he felt he was right for the part. He was ready.

When he got to the audition at a theater in London's West End, he found about a hundred other actors waiting to audition for the part. He wasn't nervous, and he felt confident. He waited for hours in the wings. Finally they called his name.

Voice: Colin Colethorpe, please.

Colin: Hello. I'm Colin Colethorpe.

Voice: Tell us about yourself, Mr. Colethorpe.

Colin: I'm a graduate of the Royal Academy. I've appeared in repertory theatre as the ghost in *Hamlet*, as Iago in *Othello* and as Lear in *King Lear*.

Voice: And before Shakespeare?

Colin: Before I did repertory, I had been working in the North. I am a dancer and a singer and I've appeared in Newcastle in *Hair* and in Leeds in *South Pacific*.

Voice: I see. Would you please wait one moment, Mr. Colethorpe?

Colin: Uh, yes.

Colin stood alone on the bare stage. It was almost silent. The director and producer and a few other people were sitting in the theater, whispering, but Colin could not see them. The spotlights were too bright. So he just stood there. He hadn't been feeling nervous before, but now he began to sweat. He didn't know what to do with his hands. He began to tremble. He shifted his weight from one foot to the other. When he thought that he had been standing there for hours, the director began to speak.

VOICE: ***Sorry, Mr. Colethorpe, we're looking for a shorter, thinner man with a deeper voice. Thank you for coming.***

Over the years, Colin went to other auditions, won some roles, and became a success. But he never forgot that experience—standing alone on that empty stage. It had taken him weeks to recover. In fact, he almost gave up acting. It was the main reason he wanted to offer his course, "Auditions and How to Survive Them." He had survived, but only barely.

WE WOULD IF WE COULD!

LESSON 67

Graduation at Colin Colethorpe's acting school is a lot of fun. The graduates put on a play. They choose the play, cast it, produce it, direct it, make the scenery, advertise, and write the programs. It is an important project because talent agents always come to see the play. And some of the students could be discovered. They could go on to movies and TV work.

Here's what Colin told them about choosing a play: "You could choose Shakespeare. That would show your classical training."

One student said, "Personally, I would want to find something more . . . more . . . uh, I mean, something broader in scope. Something with more elements of acting—comedy, singing, and dancing."

Colin said, "Well, you could choose a musical comedy or a modern drama. Or even a few one-act plays. Think about it and discuss it. Give me your answer next week. Now here is your final assignment. I would like each of you to write an essay in which you answer these two questions.

1. **If you could act in any play, which one would you choose?**
2. **If you could have written any story in history, which one would you like to have written?"**

The answers were interesting and they told Colin a lot about the students.

Here's part of what one student wrote:

If I could act in any play, I would choose The House of Bernardo Alba.[1] If I could have written any story in history, I would have written One Hundred Years of Solitude.[2]

Another student wrote:

IF I COULD BE IN ANY PLAY, I WOULD BE THE BANDIT IN RASHŌMON.[3] IF I COULD HAVE WRITTEN ANY STORY IN HISTORY, I WOULD HAVE WRITTEN THE TALE OF THE GENJI.[4]

And another student wrote:

If I could star in any play, I would be Blanche Dubois in A Streetcar Named Desire.[5] If I could have written any story in history, I would have written The Picture of Dorian Gray.[6]

[1]by Federico García Lorca, Spanish poet and dramatist, 1898–1936
[2]by Gabriel García Márquez, Colombian writer, born 1928
[3]from a short story called "In a Grove," by Ryūnosuke Akutagawa, Japanese writer and essayist, 1892–1927
[4]by Lady Shikibu Murasaki, Japanese novelist and poet, 978?–1026?
[5]by Tennessee Williams, American playwright, 1911–1983
[6]by Oscar Wilde, British author, 1854–1900

Colin was very surprised when his students told him that they had chosen *Chess*[1] for their graduation performance. *Chess* was an interesting musical that had done very well in London but hadn't done well at all in New York. It's a love story that takes place during international chess competitions in Thailand and Hungary. The chief protagonists are American and Russian. When Colin asked his students why they had chosen to produce *Chess*, here's what some of them said:

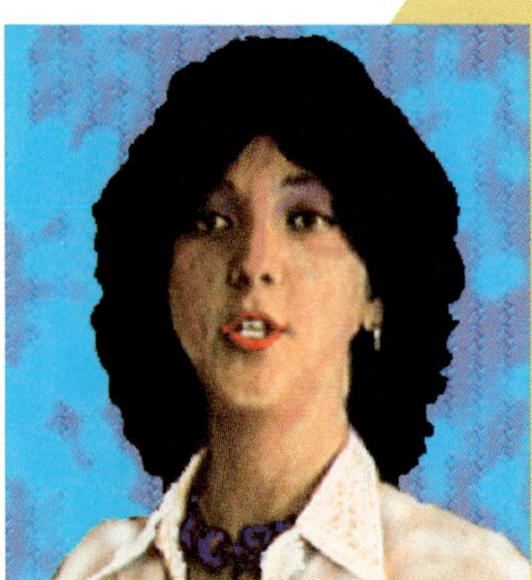

We could sing those wonderful songs. I think "One Night in Bangkok" is one of the best melodies I've ever heard.

We'd be performing a play that no one else ever performs.

We could create fabulous sets.

The cast is very large, so we would include everyone in the class.

I could practice my Russian accent.

We would attract everyone who likes the music of ABBA.

[1]A musical play written by Richard Nelson, with music written by Benny Anderson and Bjorn Ulvaeus of the Swedish rock group ABBA. The play had great success in England in the mid-1980s. It did not do very well in the United States and closed after a few months on Broadway.

I *must* have a great GOURMET caterer!

LESSON

Carol Solon and Lenny Gold took two very important steps six months ago. They got married, and they started their own catering company. And lucky for them, business is booming! They ought to write a book about their experiences. It would help people who want to start their own businesses. The problem is that most new businesses fail in the first year or two. Carol and Lenny are either smart or lucky or a little bit of both.

Carol and Lenny have known each other for a long time. They were both professors at a college in New York. Carol taught English literature, and Lenny taught psychology. They had been good friends for years. Neither of them had ever gotten married. They used to spend a lot of time together, and they often talked about the future—about what they would do when they retired from teaching. One of the things they often did together was cook. They both enjoyed it, and they appreciated good food. They used to invite friends to dinner at one of their apartments to sample their cooking. They decided that they wanted to become caterers when they retired. They became very close to each other and decided that they ought to get married. Why not? They knew each other very well, they had the same interests, they enjoyed the same things, and they had many friends in common. So they retired from teaching, got married, and began their catering business.

Their first job was to cater a graduation party at The Actor's Place. Carol had dated the director now and then, but they were just friends. In fact, Colin and Lenny became friendly. And when he needed a caterer for the party, Colin called up Carol and Lenny.

Later . . .

Lenny: How may people are going to be at Colin's party?

Carol: He thinks between 50 and 75.

Lenny: You know he really ought to be more precise.

Carol: I told him that we must have an exact number, so he said we ought to count on 75.

Lenny: OK. And what kind of party is it?

Carol: A cocktail party. But he also wants a buffet dinner. He doesn't want his guests to be hungry when they leave.

Lenny: When is it?

Carol: Soon . . . on the 14th.

Lenny: We might have a problem . . . Isn't the Bonner party the same night?

Carol: No, that's on the 16th.

Lenny: Oh, good. Well, then, what do you think we ought to serve?

Carol: Well, we'll definitely have a large selection of hors d'oeuvres, both hot and cold.

Lenny: And two or three main courses. You know, it might be interesting to have a theme. For example, we could do Japanese food, or . . .

Carol: It would be more fun, I think, to have a varied menu—lots of different international foods.

Lenny: Hey, that's a great idea. We ought to write out the menu.

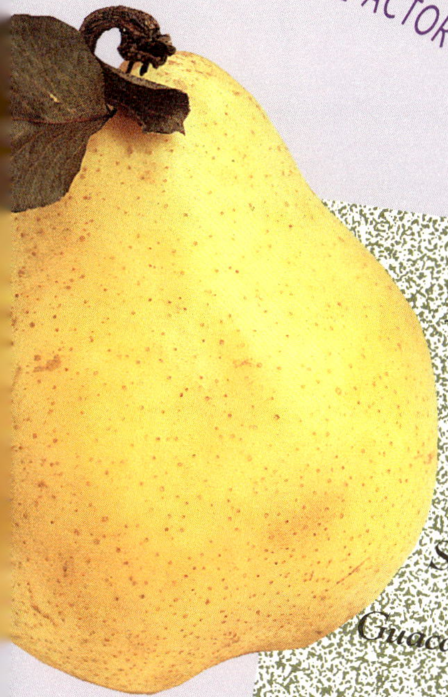

International Gourmet Menu
by Solon and Gold Catering

HORS D'OEUVRES

Sushi Mussels Vinaigrette Smoked Salmon
Sweet and Sour Shrimp
Guacamole and Tortilla Chips Miniature Shish Kebabs

MAIN COURSES

Texas Barbecued Ribs Couscous Spaghetti with Clams
Arroz con Pollo Beef Stew Pork with Snow Peas

VEGETABLES

Stir-Fried Vegetables Italian Green Beans
Potatoes in Cream Sauce

SALAD

Caesar Salad Green Salad Cole Slaw

DESSERTS

Chocolate Pudding Lemon Soufflé
Orange Sherbet Peach Cake Baklava
Apple Pie & Cheddar Cheese Fresh Fruit
Blueberry Pie Green Tea Ice Cream

69 LESSON

If we decide to get a pet, we may get a dog

About six months ago Carol and Lenny moved into a large farmhouse in the country. It has an enormous kitchen and is a perfect place to conduct their catering business. Because the house is not too far from the city, they can keep all their city customers.

Both Carol and Lenny love animals, and their new house has lots of room for a pet. But they weren't sure what kind to get because Carol loves cats and Lenny is crazy about dogs. Carol thought they could compromise and get a bird. Lenny thought it was a silly compromise and not a real solution. They did agree on one thing—they wanted to share their home with a pet. Carol had recently read an article called "Having a Pet Can Increase Your Life Span," and Lenny had heard that people with pets got fewer illnesses.

Carol: We really should do a lot of research on the kind of pet we should get.

Lenny: Why? If we want a pet, we can go to a pet store and look around.

Carol: No, I don't agree. I think we should decide. I'd like a cat.

Lenny: I know, but I'm allergic to cats.

Carol: Since when?

Lenny: Since I was a child.

Carol: If you've always been allergic to cats, how come you've never told me?

Lenny: It never came up. And since I'm allergic to cats, we ought to consider a dog. We have enough room. We could get a big one—a guard dog.

Carol: Well, OK. I'll think about it.

A few days later, Carol was talking to her friend, Kazuko Ogawa, a journalist from Japan. Kazuko often came to the States on business and always got together with Carol. This time she was staying with Carol and Lenny at their farmhouse.

Kazuko: What kind of pet are you going to get?

Carol: If we get a dog, we might get a German shepherd. Lenny wants a large one—a guard dog. I'm not sure.

Kazuko: Well, if you want a big dog, you might consider an Akita.

Carol: A what?

Kazuko: Akita. It's a very special breed in Japan.

Carol: Really? I've never heard of it. What does it look like?

Kazuko: If you have a good dictionary, it should have a picture of one.

Carol: How do you spell Akita?

Kazuko: A-K-I-T-A.

Carol: Yes, here's a drawing. It looks beautiful.

Kazuko: It is. It's a big, strong dog—about 60 centimeters high at the shoulders. And if you want a gentle but protective dog, you and Lenny should consider an Akita. We used to have one at home when I was a child.

Carol: I'd love to see one. There's a wonderful pet store nearby. They might have one.

Kazuko: I don't think so. If you want to get one, you probably have to go to a breeder. Listen, if you want to know more about Akitas, I'll send you an article I wrote about them. It's in English. And I'll send you some photos.

Carol: That would be great!

Akita-inu

If you want to know about the powerful yet gentle Akita, ask any Japanese person—adult or child. He or she will tell you the story of Hachi-Ko, a beautiful Akita who was born in Akita City in 1923. He was taken to Tokyo when he was a year old by his master, Professor Ueno, a professor in the Department of Agriculture at the Imperial University. Every morning Hachi-Ko would accompany the professor to the Shibuya train station. The professor would get on the train and Hachi-Ko would go home. But like clockwork he would be waiting for the professor at the station when the train arrived in the late afternoon. After about six months, the train arrived at the station one afternoon without the professor. Hachi-Ko waited until the last person had left the train, and then he went home. He returned the next evening to wait for the professor, who would never return. He had died the day before at the university. Hachi-Ko waited for the professor every afternoon for the rest of his life—more than ten years! He was famous and greatly loved for his loyalty and devotion. People fed him and took care of him. In 1943 a bronze statue was erected in the same spot where Hachi-Ko had waited for the professor.

Fearless and aggressive, gentle and loving, the Akita is a hunter of deer as well as a perfect baby-sitter for young children.

[1]Akita Prefecture is a region at the northern tip of Honshu Island in Japan. *Inu* = "dog."

70 LESSON

If I were BRAVE, I would do it

Nancy Jones, an editor at a reputable New York publishing company, was talking to her friend Kazuko Ogawa, a writer and journalist. Nancy was the acquisitions editor for two of Kazuko's books, and the two women became good friends. Now Nancy wanted to ask Kazuko for a favor. Nancy is a member of a women's group in New York. There are about thirty members who meet once a month in a private room at a local restaurant. Nancy knew that quite a few of the women were interested in Japanese culture. She wanted Kazuko to talk to the group about some aspect of Japanese culture. Kazuko was writing a book about the Japanese custom of appointing Living National Treasures.[1] Nancy thought that would be an especially interesting subject for her group.

Nancy was surprised when Kazuko said, "I really can't. I just don't feel comfortable speaking in public. Maybe if I had taken a course in public speaking, I could have done it. I'm fine in small groups—a book-signing party or an informal meeting. But a lecture? No, I'm sorry."

Nancy doesn't like to take no for an answer, so she asked, "What is the problem? It isn't your English, is it?"

Kazuko replied, "No, not at all. I feel comfortable speaking English. I just don't like to speak in front of large groups. I get scared—really scared. I wish I didn't. I often get requests to speak in public, but I always refuse."

Kazuko felt terrible because she didn't want to disappoint her friend. "I really feel awful about it. If I were brave, I would do it. But I'm not brave."

Nancy looked at her friend for about ten seconds. "I think you should do it. You have to get over this hurdle. And you can. Did I ever tell you about that ridiculous situation when I was afraid to drive a stick shift?"

Kazuko had never heard the story.

"Well, Andy and I decided to go to Europe for a few weeks. We wanted to visit his family in England. Then we planned to drive from London to Dover, cross the Channel to Ostend, and drive across Belgium to Germany. The problem was that I had never driven a car with a stick shift. I thought we could rent an automatic. I remember the conversation with Andy as if it were yesterday . . ."

---

[1]Certain artisans are honored by the Japanese government as the best in their field. They are responsible for preserving the traditional arts and crafts of Japan by passing on their skills to others.

"But it was a big deal! In fact it was the beginning of the worst weekend of my life," said Nancy. "I should have taken notes. It would have made a wonderful horror story about the breakup of a marriage."

"Why? What happened?" asked Kazuko. "Why was it such a problem? I've been driving a stick shift ever since I got my license."

"We all have our little fears, Kazuko. You have a problem about speaking in public," said Nancy. "For me it was a problem to drive a stick."

"Yes, I see," said Kazuko. "Go on. Tell me what happened."

"Well, Andy rented a car with a stick shift, and we went out for our first lesson early Saturday morning. He drove out to a mall on the highway. He thought I should practice in a parking lot." Nancy paused for a few seconds.

"Well, go on," said Kazuko.

But Nancy changed the subject. "Kazuko, you know what a nice man Andy is. Every woman should have a husband like him."

"Yes, he's good natured and considerate. I agree," said Kazuko. "But continue the story."

"If you had been there, you would have seen a monster! Andy was a horrible teacher. When I couldn't get the car to move in first gear, he yelled at me. When the car bounced as I shifted gears, he yelled. When I tried to shift without using the clutch, he yelled. And when I finally began to cry, he yelled again. It was horrible. If I hadn't been so upset, I would have yelled back. But I couldn't."

"So what did you do?" asked Kazuko.

"I made Andy take me home. I called a driving school, took three lessons on a stick shift, practiced on my friend's car, and was ready for our trip to Europe," said Nancy. "Now that's one fear I don't have."

Kazuko thought for a moment. Then she said, "So you think I should get over my fear of speaking in public."

"I didn't say that. But if you're asking me . . . ," said Nancy gently.

"Yes, I'm asking you," said Kazuko. She didn't really want to hear Nancy's next sentence.

"If I were you, I would try to get over this fear. Why don't you think about my women's group. They're warm and friendly people, and as I said, most of them have a special interest in Japan."

"Well, if you can do it, I guess I can try," said Kazuko. "I'll do it!"

"Great!" said Nancy. "You won't be sorry."

VOCABULARY INDEX

The Vocabulary Index includes all new words introduced in the Student Book, and related words which should be taught in the context of the lesson and Activity Book exercises. It does not include the names of people, nationalities, geographic locations, or idiomatic expressions. Two-word verbs are included when they are the focus of the lesson. The lesson number indicates where the word occurs the first time. In cases where a word appears in a later lesson with a different meaning, both lessons are listed.

ILLUSTRATION/PHOTO CREDITS

Introductory Lesson, pp. 2–3, photography: Mike Kiropford
Lesson 41, pp. 4–5, illustration: Beth Adams; p. 6, illustration: Mary McDonnell
Lesson 42, p. 7, illustration: Beth Adams; p. 8, photography: Joe Azzara/The Image Bank, Luis Villota/The Stock Market, Michael Chan/The Stock Market, Michael Quackenbush/The Image Bank, Geri Enberg/The Stock Market, Berenholtz/The Stock Market, Kunio Owaki/The Stock Market, Suzanne Brookens/The Stock Market; p. 9, NYC, Raleigh: Charles Gupton/ The Stock Market
Lesson 43, p. 10, photography: Jeff Zaruba/The Stock Market; p. 11, photography: Chiasson/Gamma Liason, S. Allen/Gamma Liason
Lesson 44, pp. 12–14, illustration: Kate Kellor
Lesson 45, pp. 15–16, illustration: Mary McDonnell
Lesson 46, pp. 17–19, illustration: Tim Grajek
Lesson 47, pp. 20, 21, illustration: Kelly Alder
Lesson 48, pp. 22–24, illustration: Andrea Barrett
Lesson 49, pp. 25–26, illustration: Lisa Blackshear
Lesson 50, pp. 27–28, illustration: Bob Eckstein
Lesson 51, pp. 30–32, illustration: Richard Truscott
Lesson 52, pp. 33–35, illustration: Ed Levine
Lesson 53, p. 36, illustration: Kate Kellor; p. 37, photography: Garvey/The Stock Market, Photofest, UPI/Bettmann; p. 38, photography: Claude Francolon/Gamma Liason, Wasser/Gamma Liason, Jill Krementz AP/Wide World Photos
Lesson 54, pp. 39–41, illustration: Donald David
Lesson 55, pp. 42–44, illustration: Richard Truscott; p. 43, photography: Steven E. Sutton/Duomo, Paul J. Sutton/Duomo, Allsport/Dave Cannon
Lesson 56, pp. 45–47, illustration: Tim Grajek
Lesson 57, pp. 48–50, illustration: Kelly Alder
Lesson 58, p. 51, illustration: Richard Truscott; p. 52, photography: Andy Caufield/The Image Bank, Blaine Harrington/The Stock Market, Henley & Savage/The Stock Market, J. Barry O'Rourke/The Stock Market
Lesson 59, p. 54, illustration: Ed Levine
Lesson 60, pp. 56–58, illustration: Lisa Blackshear
Lesson 61, p. 59, illustration: Kate Kellor and Lisa Blackshear; pp. 60–61, illustrator: Andrea Barrett
Lesson 62, pp. 62–64, illustration: Jonathan Herbert
Lesson 63, p. 65, illustration: Richard Truscott; pp. 66–67, photography: Luis Villota/The Stock Market, David Pollack/The Stock Market, Francisco Ontañon/The Image Bank, G. Anderson/The Stock Market, David Ball/The Stock Market, Fred McKinney/The Stock Market, Steve Elmore/The Stock Market, Luis Villota/The Stock Market, Paul Barton/The Stock Market, Stephen R. Brown/The Stock Market, Luis Villota/The Stock Market, Steve Dunwell/The Image Bank, John M. Roberts/The Stock Market, Jake Rajs/The Image Bank, Marvin E. Newman/The Image Bank, Jim Brown/The Stock Market, Robert Frerck/The Stock Market, Greg Davis/The Stock Market, The Image Bank, Marc Romanelli/The Image Bank, Joseph G. Standart/The Stock Market, Brett Froomer/The Image Bank, Paul Stiel/The Stock Market, J/J Clark/The Stock Market, Gary Faber/The Image Bank
Lesson 64, p. 68, illustration: Beth Adams; p. 69, illustration: Jonathan Herbert; p. 70, illustration: Beth Adams
Lesson 65, pp. 71–72, illustration: Jonathan Herbert; p. 73, illustration: Kelly Alder
Lesson 66, pp. 74–76, illustration: Ed Levine
Lesson 67, p. 77, illustration: Beth Adams; p. 78, illustration: Jonathan Herbert
Lesson 68, pp. 79–80, illustration: Beth Adams; p. 81, photography: Obremski/The Image Bank, Murray Alcosser/The Image Bank, Frank P. Rossotto/The Stock Market, Eleanor Thompson/The Stock Market
Lesson 69, p. 82, photography: Henley & Savage/The Stock Market, p. 83, illustration: Mary McDonnell; p. 84, photography: Bob Berger, Sydney Thomson/Animals, Animals, Zig Leszczynski/Animals, Animals, Jackie Flamm
Lesson 70, pp. 85–87, illustration: Bob Eckstein.